Sul H. Lee
Editor

Electronic Resources and Collection Development

Electronic Resources and Collection Development has been co-published simultaneously as *Journal of Library Administration*, Volume 36, Number 3 2002.

Pre-publication
REVIEWS,
COMMENTARIES,
EVALUATIONS . . .

"HIGHLY RECOMMENDED for college and university libraries, and any library concerned with the provision of scholarship in electronic format. VALUABLE. . . . A WELL-WRITTEN COLLECTION . . . devoted to the many issues related to building library collections in the age of ever-increasing electronic resources. . . . Provides an important overview of the challenges and opportunities facing research libraries, including collecting, storing, preserving, and selecting existing collections for digitization so that scholarly resources are available to the user in perpetuity."

Barbara I. Dewey, MA
Dean of Libraries
University of Tennessee

The Haworth Information Press
An Imprint of The Haworth Press, Inc.

Electronic Resources
and Collection Development

Electronic Resources and Collection Development has been co-published simultaneously as *Journal of Library Administration,* Volume 36, Number 3 2002.

The *Journal of Library Administration* Monographic "Separates"

Below is a list of "separates," which in serials librarianship means a special issue simultaneously published as a special journal issue or double-issue *and* as a "separate" hardbound monograph. (This is a format which we also call a "DocuSerial.")

"Separates" are published because specialized libraries or professionals may wish to purchase a specific thematic issue by itself in a format which can be separately cataloged and shelved, as opposed to purchasing the journal on an on-going basis. Faculty members may also more easily consider a "separate" for classroom adoption.

"Separates" are carefully classified separately with the major book jobbers so that the journal tie-in can be noted on new book order slips to avoid duplicate purchasing.

You may wish to visit Haworth's Website at . . .

http://www.HaworthPress.com

. . . to search our online catalog for complete tables of contents of these separates and related publications.

You may also call 1-800-HAWORTH (outside US/Canada: 607-722-5857), or Fax 1-800-895-0582 (outside US/Canada: 607-771-0012), or e-mail at:

getinfo@haworthpressinc.com

Electronic Resources and Collection Development, edited by Sul H. Lee (Vol. 36, No. 3, 2002). *Shows how electronic resources have impacted traditional collection development policies and practices.*

Information Literacy Programs: Successes and Challenges, edited by Patricia Durisin, MLIS (Vol. 36, No. 1/2, 2002). *Examines Web-based collaboration, teamwork with academic and administrative colleagues, evidence-based librarianship, and active learning strategies in library instruction programs.*

Evaluating the Twenty-First Century Library: The Association of Research Libraries New Measures Initiative, 1997-2001, edited by Donald L. DeWitt, PhD (Vol. 35, No. 4, 2001). *This collection of articles (thirteen of which previously appeared in ARL's bimonthly newsletter/ report on research issues and actions) examines the Association of Research Libraries "new measures" initiative.*

Impact of Digital Technology on Library Collections and Resource Sharing, edited by Sul H. Lee (Vol. 35, No. 3, 2001). *Shows how digital resources have changed the traditional academic library.*

Libraries and Electronic Resources: New Partnerships, New Practices, New Perspectives, edited by Pamela L. Higgins (Vol. 35, No. 1/2, 2001). *An essential guide to the Internet's impact on electronic resources management–past, present, and future.*

Diversity Now: People, Collections and Services in Academic Libraries, edited by Teresa Y. Neely, MLS, PhD, and Kuang-Hwei (Janet) Lee Smeltzer, MS, MSLIS, (Vol. 33, No. 1/2/3/4, 2001). *Examines multicultural trends in academic libraries' staff and users, types of collections, and services offered.*

Leadership in the Library and Information Science Professions: Theory and Practice, edited by Mark D. Winston, MLS, PhD (Vol. 32, No. 3/4, 2001). *Offers fresh ideas for developing and using leadership skills, including recruiting potential leaders, staff training and development, issues of gender and ethnic diversity, and budget strategies for success.*

Off-Campus Library Services, edited by Ann Marie Casey (Vol. 31, No. 3/4, 2001 and Vol. 32, No. 1/2, 2001). *This informative volume examines various aspects of off-campus, or distance learning. It explores training issues for library staff, Web site development, changing roles for librarians, the uses of conferencing software, library support for Web-based courses, library agreements and how to successfully negotiate them, and much more!*

Research Collections and Digital Information, edited by Sul H. Lee (Vol. 31, No. 2, 2000). *Offers new strategies for collecting, organizing, and accessing library materials in the digital age.*

Academic Research on the Internet: Options for Scholars & Libraries, edited by Helen Laurence, MLS, EdD, and William Miller, MLS, PhD (Vol. 30, No. 1/2/3/4, 2000). *"Emphasizes quality over quantity. . . . Presents the reader with the best research-oriented Web sites in the field. A state-of-the-art review of academic use of the Internet as well as a guide to the best Internet sites and services. . . . A useful addition for any academic library." (David A. Tyckoson, MLS, Head of Reference, California State University, Fresno)*

Management for Research Libraries Cooperation, edited by Sul H. Lee (Vol. 29, No. 3/4, 2000). *Delivers sound advice, models, and strategies for increasing sharing between institutions to maximize the amount of printed and electronic research material you can make available in your library while keeping costs under control.*

Integration in the Library Organization, edited by Christine E. Thompson, PhD (Vol. 29, No. 2, 1999). *Provides librarians with the necessary tools to help libraries balance and integrate public and technical services and to improve the capability of libraries to offer patrons quality services and large amounts of information.*

Library Training for Staff and Customers, edited by Sara Ramser Beck, MLS, MBA (Vol. 29, No. 1, 1999). *This comprehensive book is designed to assist library professionals involved in presenting or planning training for library staff members and customers. You will explore ideas for effective general reference training, training on automated systems, training in specialized subjects such as African American history and biography, and training for areas such as patents and trademarks, and business subjects.* Library Training for Staff and Customers *answers numerous training questions and is an excellent guide for planning staff development.*

Collection Development in the Electronic Environment: Shifting Priorities, edited by Sul H. Lee (Vol. 28, No. 4, 1999). *Through case studies and firsthand experiences, this volume discusses meeting the needs of scholars at universities, budgeting issues, user education, staffing in the electronic age, collaborating libraries and resources, and how vendors meet the needs of different customers.*

The Age Demographics of Academic Librarians: A Profession Apart, by Stanley J. Wilder (Vol. 28, No. 3, 1999). *The average age of librarians has been increasing dramatically since 1990. This unique book will provide insights on how this demographic issue can impact a library and what can be done to make the effects positive.*

Collection Development in a Digital Environment, edited by Sul H. Lee (Vol. 28, No. 1, 1999). *Explores ethical and technological dilemmas of collection development and gives several suggestions on how a library can successfully deal with these challenges and provide patrons with the information they need.*

Scholarship, Research Libraries, and Global Publishing, by Jutta Reed-Scott (Vol. 27, No. 3/4, 1999). *This book documents a research project in conjunction with the Association of Research Libraries (ARL) that explores the issue of foreign acquisition and how it affects collection in international studies, area studies, collection development, and practices of international research libraries.*

Managing Multicultural Diversity in the Library: Principles and Issues for Administrators, edited by Mark Winston (Vol. 27, No. 1/2, 1999). *Defines diversity, clarifies why it is important to address issues of diversity, and identifies goals related to diversity and how to go about achieving those goals.*

Information Technology Planning, edited by Lori A. Goetsch (Vol. 26, No. 3/4, 1999). *Offers innovative approaches and strategies useful in your library and provides some food for thought about information technology as we approach the millennium.*

The Economics of Information in the Networked Environment, edited by Meredith A. Butler, MLS, and Bruce R. Kingma, PhD (Vol. 26, No. 1/2, 1998). *"A book that should be read both by information professionals and by administrators, faculty and others who share a collective concern to provide the most information to the greatest number at the lowest cost in the networked environment." (Thomas J. Galvin, PhD, Professor of Information Science and Policy, University at Albany, State University of New York)*

OCLC 1967-1997: Thirty Years of Furthering Access to the World's Information, edited by K. Wayne Smith (Vol. 25, No. 2/3/4, 1998). *"A rich–and poignantly personal, at times–historical account of what is surely one of this century's most important developments in librarianship." (Deanna B. Marcum, PhD, President, Council on Library and Information Resources, Washington, DC)*

Management of Library and Archival Security: From the Outside Looking In, edited by Robert K. O'Neill, PhD (Vol. 25, No. 1, 1998). *"Provides useful advice and on-target insights for professionals caring for valuable documents and artifacts." (Menzi L. Behrnd-Klodt, JD, Attorney/Archivist, Klodt and Associates, Madison, WI)*

Economics of Digital Information: Collection, Storage, and Delivery, edited by Sul H. Lee (Vol. 24, No. 4, 1997). *Highlights key concepts and issues vital to a library's successful venture into the digital environment and helps you understand why the transition from the printed page to the digital packet has been problematic for both creators of proprietary materials and users of those materials.*

The Academic Library Director: Reflections on a Position in Transition, edited by Frank D'Andraia, MLS (Vol. 24, No. 3, 1997). *"A useful collection to have whether you are seeking a position as director or conducting a search for one." (College & Research Libraries News)*

Emerging Patterns of Collection Development in Expanding Resource Sharing, Electronic Information, and Network Environment, edited by Sul H. Lee (Vol. 24, No. 1/2, 1997). *"The issues it deals with are common to us all. We all need to make our funds go further and our resources work harder, and there are ideas here which we can all develop." (The Library Association Record)*

Interlibrary Loan/Document Delivery and Customer Satisfaction: Strategies for Redesigning Services, edited by Pat L. Weaver-Meyers, Wilbur A. Stolt, and Yem S. Fong (Vol. 23, No. 1/2, 1997). *"No interlibrary loan department supervisor at any mid-sized to large college or university library can afford not to read this book." (Gregg Sapp, MLS, MEd, Head of Access Services, University of Miami, Richter Library, Coral Gables, Florida)*

Access, Resource Sharing and Collection Development, edited by Sul H. Lee (Vol. 22, No. 4, 1996). *Features continuing investigation and discussion of important library issues, specifically the role of libraries in acquiring, storing, and disseminating information in different formats.*

Managing Change in Academic Libraries, edited by Joseph J. Branin (Vol. 22, No. 2/3, 1996). *"Touches on several aspects of academic library management, emphasizing the changes that are occurring at the present time. . . . Recommended this title for individuals or libraries interested in management aspects of academic libraries." (RQ American Library Association)*

Libraries and Student Assistants: Critical Links, edited by William K. Black, MLS (Vol. 21, No. 3/4, 1995). *"A handy reference work on many important aspects of managing student assistants. . . . Solid, useful information on basic management issues in this work and several chapters are useful for experienced managers." (The Journal of Academic Librarianship)*

The Future of Resource Sharing, edited by Shirley K. Baker and Mary E. Jackson, MLS (Vol. 21, No. 1/2, 1995). *"Recommended for library and information science schools because of its balanced presentation of the ILL/document delivery issues." (Library Acquisitions: Practice and Theory)*

The Future of Information Services, edited by Virginia Steel, MA, and C. Brigid Welch, MLS (Vol. 20, No. 3/4, 1995). *"The leadership discussions will be useful for library managers as will the discussions of how library structures and services might work in the next century." (Australian Special Libraries)*

The Dynamic Library Organizations in a Changing Environment, edited by Joan Giesecke, MLS, DPA (Vol. 20, No. 2, 1995). *"Provides a significant look at potential changes in the library world and presents its readers with possible ways to address the negative results of such changes. . . . Covers the key issues facing today's libraries . . . Two thumbs up!" (Marketing Library Resources)*

Access, Ownership, and Resource Sharing, edited by Sul H. Lee (Vol. 20, No. 1, 1995). *The contributing authors present a useful and informative look at the current status of information provision and some of the challenges the subject presents.*

Libraries as User-Centered Organizations: Imperatives for Organizational Change, edited by Meredith A. Butler (Vol. 19, No. 3/4, 1994). *"Presents a very timely and well-organized discussion of major trends and influences causing organizational changes." (Science Books & Films)*

Declining Acquisitions Budgets: Allocation, Collection Development and Impact Communication, edited by Sul H. Lee (Vol. 19, No. 2, 1994). *"Expert and provocative. . . . Presents many ways of looking at library budget deterioration and responses to it . . . There is much food for thought here." (Library Resources & Technical Services)*

The Role and Future of Special Collections in Research Libraries: British and American Perspectives, edited by Sul H. Lee (Vol. 19, No. 1, 1993). *"A provocative but informative read for library users, academic administrators, and private sponsors." (International Journal of Information and Library Research)*

Catalysts for Change: Managing Libraries in the 1990s, edited by Gisela M. von Dran, DPA, MLS, and Jennifer Cargill, MSLS, MSed (Vol. 18, No. 3/4, 1994). *"A useful collection of articles which focuses on the need for librarians to employ enlightened management practices in order to adapt to and thrive in the rapidly changing information environment." (Australian Library Review)*

Monographic "Separates" list continued at the back

Electronic Resources
and Collection Development

Sul H. Lee
Editor

Electronic Resources and Collection Development has been
co-published simultaneously as *Journal of Library Administration*,
Volume 36, Number 3 2002.

The Haworth Information Press
An Imprint of
The Haworth Press, Inc.
New York • London • Oxford

Published by

The Haworth Information Press®, 10 Alice Street, Binghamton, NY 13904-1580 USA

The Haworth Information Press® is an imprint of The Haworth Press, Inc., 10 Alice Street, Binghamton, NY 13904-1580 USA.

Electronic Resources and Collection Development has been co-published simultaneously as *Journal of Library Administration,* Volume 36, Number 3 2002.

The development, preparation, and publication of this work has been undertaken with great care. However, the publisher, employees, editors, and agents of The Haworth Press and all imprints of The Haworth Press, Inc., including The Haworth Medical Press® and Pharmaceutical Products Press®, are not responsible for any errors contained herein or for consequences that may ensue from use of materials or information contained in this work. Opinions expressed by the author(s) are not necessarily those of The Haworth Press, Inc. With regard to case studies, identities and circumstances of individuals discussed herein have been changed to protect confidentiality. Any resemblance to actual persons, living or dead, is entirely coincidental.

Cover design by Jennifer M. Gaska.

Library of Congress Cataloging-in-Publication Data

University of Oklahoma. Libraries. Conference (2002 : Oklahoma City, Okla.)
Electronic resources and collection development / Sul H. Lee, editor.
p. cm.
Papers originally presented at the 2002 University of Oklahoma Libraries Annual Conference held in Oklahoma City.
Co-published simultaneously as Journal of library administration, v. 36, no. 3, 2002.
Includes bibliographical references and index.
ISBN 0-7890-2068-8 (alk. paper) – ISBN 0-7890-2069-6 (pbk : alk. paper)
1. Academic libraries–Collection development–United States–Congresses. 2. Libraries–United States–Special collections–Electronic information resources–Congresses. I. Lee, Sul H. II. Journal of library administration. III. Title.
Z675.U5 U577 2002
025.2'187'0973–dc21
2002152856

Indexing, Abstracting & Website/Internet Coverage

This section provides you with a list of major indexing & abstracting services. That is to say, each service began covering this periodical during the year noted in the right column. Most Websites which are listed below have indicated that they will either post, disseminate, compile, archive, cite or alert their own Website users with research-based content from this work. (This list is as current as the copyright date of this publication.)

Abstracting, Website/Indexing Coverage . . . . Year When Coverage Began

- *Academic Abstracts/CD-ROM* 1993
- *Academic Search: data base of 2,000 selected academic serials,*
  updated monthly: EBSCO Publishing 1995
- *Academic Search Elite (EBSCO)* 1993
- *Academic Search Premier (EBSCO)* 2001
- *AGRICOLA Database <www.natl.usda.gov/ag98>* 1991
- *Business ASAP* 1993
- *CNPIEC Reference Guide: Chinese National Directory*
  of Foreign Periodicals 1995
- *Current Articles on Library Literature and Services (CALLS)* 1992
- *Current Cites [Digital Libraries] [Electronic Publishing] [Multimedia &*
  Hypermedia] [Networks & Networking] [General] 2000
- *Current Index to Journals in Education* 1986
- *Educational Administration Abstracts (EAA)* 1991
- *FINDEX <www.publist.com>* 1999
- *FRANCIS. INIST/CNRS <www.inist.fr>* 1986
- *General BusinessFile ASAP <www.galegroup.com>* 1993
- *General Reference Center GOLD on InfoTrac Web* 1984
- *Higher Education Abstracts, providing the latest in research & theory in more*
  than 140 major topics 1991
- *IBZ International Bibliography of Periodical Literature <www.saur.de>* 1995

(continued)

Special Bibliographic Notes related to special journal issues (separates) and indexing/abstracting:

- indexing/abstracting services in this list will also cover material in any "separate" that is co-published simultaneously with Haworth's special thematic journal issue or DocuSerial. Indexing/abstracting usually covers material at the article/chapter level.
- monographic co-editions are intended for either non-subscribers or libraries which intend to purchase a second copy for their circulating collections.
- monographic co-editions are reported to all jobbers/wholesalers/approval plans. The source journal is listed as the "series" to assist the prevention of duplicate purchasing in the same manner utilized for books-in-series.
- to facilitate user/access services all indexing/abstracting services are encouraged to utilize the co-indexing entry note indicated at the bottom of the first page of each article/chapter/contribution.
- this is intended to assist a library user of any reference tool (whether print, electronic, online, or CD-ROM) to locate the monographic version if the library has purchased this version but not a subscription to the source journal.
- individual articles/chapters in any Haworth publication are also available through the Haworth Document Delivery Service (HDDS).

For Melissa

Electronic Resources
and Collection Development

CONTENTS

ABOUT THE EDITOR

Sul H. Lee, PhD, Dean of the University Libraries, University of Oklahoma, is an internationally recognized leader and consultant in the library administration and management field. Dean Lee is a past member of the Association of Research Libraries Board of Directors, the ARL Office of Management Services Advisory Committee, and the Council for the American Library Association. His works include *The Impact of Rising Costs of Serials and Monographs on Library Services and Programs*; *Library Material Costs and Access to Information*; *Budgets for Acquisitions: Strategies for Serials, Monographs, and Electronic Formats*; *Vendor Evaluation and Acquisition Budgets*; *The Role and Future of Special Collections in Research Libraries*; *Declining Acquisitions Budgets*; and *Access, Ownership, and Resource Sharing*. He is Editor of the *Journal of Library Administration*.

Introduction

Sul H. Lee

The transition to electronic resources in academic libraries is gaining momentum in the opening years of the 21st century. Collection development librarians are acquiring digital materials for their institutions in record numbers, and the convenience that digital resources offer is helping to tip the scales in favor of access in the "ownership versus access" debate in academic librarianship.

Electronic resources and collection development in academic libraries was the theme for the 2002 University of Oklahoma Libraries annual conference held in Oklahoma City on March 7th and 8th. Nine national library leaders shared their perspectives on the changes that electronic resources have brought to collection development policies and practices of research libraries. Their papers are presented in this publication, much as they were delivered at the conference.

Jay Jordan, president of Online Computer Library Center, opened the conference by examining some of the electronic resource-related trends and initiatives now underway in libraries. He noted that e-books were making strong inroads on collection development policy and foresees continuing demand for digital resources as librarians seek to improve access for their users.

In her presentation, Jennifer A. Younger, University Librarian at Notre Dame University, went a step further by declaring that electronic resources have turned the corner and overtaken print materials in academic libraries. She considers access the driving force in contemporary collection development strategies and she offers compelling examples of how electronic resources are influencing traditional collection development patterns.

[Haworth co-indexing entry note]: "Introduction." Lee, Sul H. Co-published simultaneously in *Journal of Library Administration* (The Haworth Information Press, an imprint of The Haworth Press, Inc.) Vol. 36, No. 3, 2002, pp. 1-3; and: *Electronic Resources and Collection Development* (ed: Sul H. Lee) The Haworth Information Press, an imprint of The Haworth Press, Inc., 2002, pp. 1-3. Single or multiple copies of this article are available for a fee from The Haworth Document Delivery Service [1-800-HAWORTH, 9:00 a.m. - 5:00 p.m. (EST). E-mail address: getinfo@haworthpressinc.com].

Taking a slightly more conservative approach, Barbara McFadden Allen, director, the Committee on Institutional Cooperation, a consortium of twelve midwestern teaching and research universities, presents her views of how senior university administrators perceive the 21st century library. She advocates maintaining a balance between the opportunities digital resources offer and the obligation to develop and preserve the more traditional collections in research libraries.

Just a short generation ago, the library was the place to go to find information and research materials about most subjects. Dennis Dillon, head of collections and information resources at the University of Texas, Austin, however, suggests that the library may no longer be the best place to find many kinds of information. He examines how libraries might respond to this changing environment, avoid some of the pitfalls of digital information acquisition, and still retain their place and mission in academia.

Distance education is another rapidly growing service area for academic libraries. Anne Marie Casey, Central Michigan University's director for off-campus library services, calls attention to the proliferation of distant learning programs in higher education and the ensuing need for academic libraries to support those programs. Her article reviews the issues and challenges inherent in collection development for distance learning programs.

William J. Crowe, Spencer Librarian at the University of Kansas, offers a different perspective on digital resources in libraries. He recalls that earlier generations of librarians were frequently learned bookmen and keenly interested in the manuscript resources in their libraries and special collections. He suggests that contemporary librarians have lost contact with the rare book and manuscript collections within their libraries, and calls for a revisiting of special collections in research libraries for the potential they offer for digital conversion and improved access of these unique resources.

The Association of Research Libraries (ARL) has long been a leader in promoting access to library resources and Mary E. Jackson, senior program officer for access services at ARL, reports on the progress of ARL's Scholars Portal Initiative. Her article reviews the five-fold services that the portal provides.

Sarah E. Thomas, Cornell University Librarian, notes that the advance of digital resources has not stopped research libraries from building their own localized collections tailored to local research interests and programs. While reviewing past failed cooperative collection development ventures, she suggests that local specialized collections be digitized and made available to the scholarly community through collectively supported Web sites.

JSTOR president, Kevin M. Guthrie, concluded the conference by presenting some of the data JSTOR has collected about who uses electronic journals, how they are used, what disciplines favor electronic resources, and how these newly defined use patterns may affect electronic collection development in the future.

While diverse in content and conclusions, all of these papers share common ground in that they offer new insights on how libraries are meeting the challenge of reshaping collection development programs with electronic resources. As with past conferences, the papers stimulated lively discussion in their sessions. It is my hope that the publication of these articles will continue to provoke thought and further discussion within the library profession. I want to thank all of the authors for their thoughtful contributions. I also want to thank Dr. Donald L. DeWitt, curator of the University of Oklahoma Libraries Western History Collections, for his assistance in compiling this work.

New Directions
in Electronic Collection Development

Jay Jordan

SUMMARY. The author reviews current trends in the development of collections of electronic resources and discusses initiatives under way in the library community. *[Article copies available for a fee from The Haworth Document Delivery Service: 1-800-HAWORTH. E-mail address: <getinfo@haworth pressinc.com> Website: <http://www.HaworthPress.com> © 2002 by The Haworth Press, Inc. All rights reserved.]*

KEYWORDS. Collection development, electronic resources, OCLC, Vannevar Bush, Tim Berners-Lee

Good afternoon. In my remarks today, I will discuss some trends in collection development and management of electronic resources as well as some initiatives involving my organization, OCLC. Indeed, in my presentation, I will be looking at collection development through OCLC-tinted glasses, that is, from the perspective of our global cooperative of some 41,000 libraries in 81 countries. The members of our cooperative are grappling with these issues and challenges, and we at OCLC are getting involved as well.

First, what are the trends in electronic collection development and management? What are the drivers? Where is this part of the library profession headed? A brief survey of the library literature turned up some pretty interesting quotations. Let me share a few of them with you.

Jay Jordan is President and CEO, OCLC.

[Haworth co-indexing entry note]: "New Directions in Electronic Collection Development." Jordan, Jay. Co-published simultaneously in *Journal of Library Administration* (The Haworth Information Press, an imprint of The Haworth Press, Inc.) Vol. 36, No. 3, 2002, pp. 5-17; and: *Electronic Resources and Collection Development* (ed: Sul H. Lee) The Haworth Information Press, an imprint of The Haworth Press, Inc., 2002, pp. 5-17. Single or multiple copies of this article are available for a fee from The Haworth Document Delivery Service [1-800-HAWORTH, 9:00 a.m. - 5:00 p.m. (EST). E-mail address: getinfo@haworthpressinc.com].

The Web and the electronic journal are deconstructing the serials landscape. Scholars can now publish without publishers, publishers can distribute without vendors, and end-users can get access to the scholarly literature without going through the library.[1]

Selectors creating subject Web pages are not so much building collections as creating paths out of their collections to resources provided elsewhere.[2]

[Developing a collection of electronic resources is] like foraging in the jungle; a trackless, vine-tangled wilderness full of unknown species, some of which look appetizing but may be poisonous . . . The librarian collecting electronic resources is not a harvester of cultivated crops but a hunter and gatherer of wild fruit and other treasures.[3]

The role of the bibliographer is changing from that of developing the local collection to that of mapping the existence of materials and how they are accessed.[4]

Obviously, collection development librarians are facing what appear to be, to paraphrase Pogo, some insurmountable opportunities. The more things change, though, the more they remain the same. The traditional selection criteria of quality, library relevancy, aesthetics and cost are as relevant today as they have always been. Now, however, these criteria include such aspects as quality of the interface and the search engine, vendor reliability and licensing considerations.

The library's traditional role of acquiring, organizing, providing access to, and preserving knowledge and information and passing it on to future generations has never been more important, and at the same time, it has never been more in question, thanks to the World Wide Web.

In 10 years, the World Wide Web has wrought enormous changes in libraries. Those changes are best summed up in an anecdote that appeared recently in the *Columbus Dispatch*, which is the daily newspaper in our area back at OCLC. Roger Blackwell, a professor of marketing at The Ohio State University, and, I am proud to say, also a member of the faculty of the OCLC/Ohio State University Center for Leadership Development, is quoted: "Ten years ago, I was challenging students to get out of the library and go to the Web to learn. Now, I have to force them to get off the Internet to actually see that a library has something to offer."[5] As I frequently point out to Professor Blackwell, libraries have not been standing still during this past decade of the Web. This audience needs no retelling of our ongoing efforts to manage both print and electronic collections as we build our digital libraries of the 21st century. Perhaps Ann Okerson said it most succinctly when she stated that:

> Today we find ourselves moving into a user-centered, rather than a collection-centered, world. Librarians are already finding that their mission lies in customizing information for their users–and publishers are seeing a similar role for themselves.[6]

Ann also makes the important point that librarians should work with users to integrate electronic resources of all kinds into research and education as rapidly as feasible. Part of that challenge is maintaining a balance and interaction among information sources.

No discussion of trends in collection development would be complete without mentioning two persons outside librarianship whose ideas have greatly influenced the direction of collection development. They are Vannevar Bush and Tim Berners-Lee.

VANNEVAR BUSH

It seems to me that Vannevar Bush was a crypto-collection development librarian. Most of you will recall that Bush was a distinguished scientist. He was the first Director of the Office of Scientific Research & Development when it was founded in 1941. He wrote the report that resulted in the Manhattan Project. He had significant influence in establishing the National Science Foundation in 1951. He was essentially the first Science Czar. Bush was among the first to articulate what would become known as the Information Explosion. In 1945, his seminal essay, "As We May Think," appeared in the *Atlantic Monthly*. In that article he outlined a photo-electro-mechanical machine that he called the Memex. It was a desktop machine that would display text and pictures (from a microfilm library) at the press of a button. Users would create trails of knowledge along storable links, much like today's Web surfers. Bush called it an enlarged intimate supplement to his memory. That article has been read and reread by the people who have shaped the digital age we now live in, including the other mega-force on collection development trends, Tim Berners-Lee.

TIM BERNERS-LEE

Tim Berners-Lee was a software engineer at CERN, the European Laboratory for Particle Physics, in Geneva, Switzerland. Like Vannevar Bush, he was interested in programs that dealt with information in a brain-like way. For example, in 1980, he developed some software named Enquire, which was short for a Victorian-era encyclopedia from childhood that had the wonderful name, "Enquire Within Upon Everything."

In 1989, he proposed a global hypertext project called the World Wide Web. Then, he developed HyperText Markup Language. He designed an addressing scheme that gave each Web page a unique location–the URL. Then he came up with rules that permitted these documents to be linked–HyperText Transfer Protocol. Or, HTTP for short. Then he created one of the first browser/editors for the Web. (It was called Apache.)

You can read how Berners-Lee did all this in a book he wrote called *Weaving the Web*. Its subtitle is "The Original Design and Ultimate Destiny of the World Wide Web by Its Inventor." I was struck by two things in the book. First, Berners-Lee was not engaged in a formal project to "invent the Web." He was hacking around on company time. It started out as connecting an online phone book for the CERN particle physics research center to different desktops among the researchers there. And, over time and experimentation, it evolved into the Web. And second, while Berners-Lee was certainly into deep technology, his vision was more about knowledge and society. Indeed, he wrote, "The Web is more a social creation than a technical one. I designed it for a social effect–to help people work together–and not as a technical toy."[7] As we all know, the Web is transforming business, commerce, education, indeed, most aspects of our lives.

However, we are only at the beginning of this transformation. As Berners-Lee points out, to date, the Web "has developed most rapidly as a medium of documents for people rather than of information that can be manipulated automatically. By augmenting Web pages with data targeted at computers and by adding documents solely for computers, we will transform the Web into the Semantic Web." According to Berners-Lee, in the world of the Semantic Web, computers will find the meaning of semantic data by following hyperlinks to definitions of key terms and rules for reasoning about them logically. The resulting infrastructure will spur the development of automated Web services such as highly functional agents. Ordinary users will compose Semantic Web pages and add new definitions and rules using off-the-shelf software that will assist with semantic markup. "The real power of the Semantic Web will be realized when people create many programs that collect Web content from diverse sources, process the information and exchange the results with other programs."[8]

"A typical process will involve the creation of a 'value chain' in which subassemblies of information are passed from one agent to another, each one 'adding value,' to construct the final product requested by the end-user."[9]

This is a world that aligns with the trends that I mentioned at the beginning of this paper. The landscape is being creatively deconstructed and rebuilt into a user-centric model.

Today, I would like to share with you two initiatives that are under way at OCLC that have implication for collection management and development. The first initiative is with e-books and netLibrary. The second involves a new organization and new services to help libraries digitize and preserve their collections.

netLIBRARY

As you may know, on January 25, OCLC acquired the assets of netLibrary, a company in Boulder, Colorado that in three years had become one of the leading providers of e-books. Indeed, in terms of providing e-books specifically to the library market, netLibrary is the leading provider at present.

About 6,600 libraries presently use netLibrary eBook content and tools. Fourteen of our 16 U.S. Regional Network affiliates have arrangements for libraries in their regions to purchase netLibrary resources. There are 40,000 titles in the netLibrary collection. These digital resources complement the 3,700 e-journals from 62 publishers in OCLC FirstSearch Electronic Collections Online. We expect that access to e-books will enhance the capabilities of OCLC's forthcoming 24 × 7 reference service. We also believe that netLibrary's collection, with requisite agreements with publishers, will be an important addition to OCLC's forthcoming digital archive.

Today, I thought you might find it interesting to hear a little bit about the collection development policy of netLibrary and some e-book usage statistics from libraries that were reported at the ALA Midwinter Meeting and Conference in New Orleans.

netLibrary's collection development policy is posted on its Web site. I invite you to visit the site and read the policy. The policy is intended to be not only a planning and management tool, but also a communication tool. It provides information to netLibrary users about what may and may not be expected to be found within the collection.

The netLibrary collection of e-books can support libraries serving colleges, universities, junior colleges and vocational schools. Let me share with you a few of the salient points in the policy that pertain to academic libraries.

1. netLibrary follows collection development guidelines established by the Research Libraries Group (RLG) and adopted for the North American Collections Inventory Project. Additionally, the direction and focus of collection development at netLibrary is influenced by usage data, surveys, and focus groups with academic and public librarians.
2. netLibrary attempts to collect materials that are most current and authoritative within every subject and as defined in the RLG Conspectus. Acquisition of materials will be decided on the basis of currency, authority, research value and enduring value.
3. netLibrary intends to support the mission of higher education institutions with e-books that complement and enhance library service to students on and off campus and through distance education programs.
4. netLibrary e-books are intended to support curricula in the fields of: business administration, library science, education, nursing, computer science, and engineering.

netLibrary recently introduced TitleSelect, which is a new resource that gives you access to netLibrary's entire catalog of some 40,000 e-book titles. This useful interactive instrument now allows you to select titles individually, create title lists and order e-books that best fit your specific library needs. You can build your collection lists through multiple search tools, save them for future edits, and share them with colleagues. Once your title list is determined, you simply submit the order for processing.

Going forward, content acquisition will continue to be driven by the needs expressed by users. netLibrary will continue to work with publishers to obtain desired content and deliver it to users when and where they need it. netLibrary will continue to create packaged collections tailored to the needs of academic, public and special libraries.

netLibrary staff have been working with libraries to track, measure and draw conclusions from the presence and use of e-books. The November 2001 issue of *College & Research Libraries* includes a paper entitled "Life Cycle Costs of Library Collections: Creation of Effective Performance and Cost Metrics for Library Resources."[10] The authors concluded that the cost of maintaining a monograph in a collection over a 50-year period can be as much as seven times the initial cost of the title.

Elsewhere, a body of research on e-books is starting to develop in the library literature. For example, in a recent issue of *Collection Building*, librarians at Texas A&Ms experience in joining 91 other members of AMIGOS in purchasing a basic collection of 10,000 e-books through netLibrary in October 1999. The authors' analyzed usage over a 270-day period and made some conclusions that are consistent with what others are finding. It should come as no surprise that loading MARC records into the OPAC and promoting availability of e-books locally increased usage dramatically. The authors also expressed such concerns as: price of e-books, archive questions, subject matter influences, copyright and willingness of users to adopt e-books.[11]

At the 2002 ALA Midwinter Meeting and Conference, two netLibrary users reported on their experiences with e-books.

Marion County (Indiana) Internet Public Library reported that in three years, they reduced the loan period from three weeks to 72 hours. The most-used titles in their 4,000 title collection were the "Complete Idiot's Guide" series, and computer science and reference titles. The e-books enabled the library to provide materials that it could not easily provide in print. These titles are often checked-out or missing from the library shelves, making them unavailable to patrons.

The California State University System conducted a pilot program in 2001 with netLibrary involving the 23 campuses and a $100,000 budget for e-books. Staff developed guidelines for collection development. CSU system staff concluded that e-books are preferable for high-use, short-lived titles. Materials that fall into this category include reference works, computer manuals and some business books. They also noted that these subject areas receive the highest level of usage in e-book collections.

At the presentation at ALA Midwinter, Dr. Connaway noted that as e-book technology continues to evolve, it is becoming increasingly clear that library patrons want access to information and not devices. Users do not read e-books from cover to cover; instead, they consult them. They search e-books for desired information and then put the e-book back on the electronic shelf.

It is also becoming increasingly clear that e-books have a definite place in the emerging digital library. And, I think that OCLC and its member libraries have an opportunity to help shape the development of the e-book.

In 1998, OCLC Founder Fred Kilgour, at the age of 84, published a book with Oxford University Press. Its title is *The Evolution of the Book*. Fred made an interesting observation about the utility of e-books. Let me read it to you.

The unacceptability of the present electronic book is often expressed in what has come to be known as the 'can't curl up in bed with it' syndrome, closely followed by the 'can't read it at the beach' complaint. Both protests are valid, but it may be supposed that advances in technology and design will soon overcome these insufficiencies as they have overcome others in the history of the book. After all, second- and third-century codices, many a foot or more tall, hardly constituted bedfellows, any more than did the seventeen-inch tall 42-line Gutenberg Bible, or the taller-than-a foot folios that followed in 1457, 1459, 1460 and 1462.

Fred goes on to describe six specifications that an e-book needs to be acceptable, including, "it should be able to access text in any one of millions of databases anywhere and at any time."[12] As usual, Fred is way ahead of the curve!

DIGITAL AND PRESERVATION RESOURCES

We are launching three major initiatives in our new Digital and Preservation Services area. First, in response to requests from the library community, we are establishing a digital co-op as a resource for libraries and institutions seeking to digitize, preserve and publish electronic collections. It will help libraries gain funding and share information on digitization projects. Second, in the coming year, we will introduce a digital archive that will provide long-term retention and access for digital content. Objects in the archive will be cataloged and indexed for end-user searching and retrieval through WorldCat. And third, we provide a full range of superior digitization and preservation microfilming processes through preservation resource centers. In short, we are providing a complete, integrated solution for managing digital collections.

Digital Co-Op

The Digital Co-op will serve as an administrative home for ongoing collaborative programs. Librarians from these institutions are going to be learning about and sharing best practices in digitization and preservation. The Co-op serves as a clearinghouse for grant information, grant development services, and consultation on grant management.

Co-op participants have access to advisory groups of subject experts from the Co-op, and OCLC specialists are available to consult on topics such as selection for preservation and digitization, preservation of collections, digitization and metadata creation, and rights management. Engaging in cooperative projects will increase reference and research access to your own resources as well as to the resources of other institutions.

Co-op participants will also be able to explore the capabilities of CONTENTdm, which is software that provides a complete set of media asset management tools to assist with every phase of digital collection development and administration, from storing media items to customizing access options. As a Co-op participant, you determine who can access your digitized collections. Collections can be made available to a broad audience through OCLC FirstSearch. This will increase the visibility of your institution and help you demonstrate the value of your digitization efforts to your funding sources. And, we hope, it will increase the likelihood of winning funding and reduce your cost of funding.

Clearly, the Digital Co-op represents an exciting new chapter in cooperative collection development.

Digital Archive

In considering storage of digital collections, libraries are faced with numerous physical preservation and intellectual property decisions. Is the collection being stored as "back-up" protection or is ongoing access required? Is access today all that's important, or is it critical that the collection be accessible over the long-term, even if its format has become outdated? Does the library retain the rights to provide access to the collection, or relinquish those rights to a third party? Does the library have long-term access to electronic collections they have licensed if the creator ceases to support the content?

In designing the Digital Archive, OCLC has built in the flexibility for libraries to choose the type of storage needed for each collection so that libraries don't pay for more than they need for that specific collection. Libraries and other e-content creators can choose to have "continual access" to frequently accessed collections or "dark storage" as back up for collections stored for ongoing access on their own or someone else's server. Libraries retain the rights to their collections, controlling access to them and deciding if collections are available only to their constituents, to select groups, or to the entire worldwide community accessing WorldCat. For long-term preservation, the Digital Archive will offer format protection service, providing ongoing management of technological changes to ensure continued access to documents as formats are abandoned or changed over time (e.g., reading an HTML document 20 years from now).

The OCLC Digital Archive will be part of the growing network of digital repositories accessible via the Web. Collections in the Archive will consist of information that has been created electronically or reborn digitally, paper-based collections and other analog formats such as video or audio that have been or will be converted to digital formats, and born-digital collections such as e-journals and e-books. Access to the collections in The Archive will be from library catalogs, OCLC FirstSearch, and other Web indexes.

The OCLC Digital Archive protects the investment your institution has made in digitizing your collections. By contracting with OCLC for the specific services you need, you don't have to be dependent upon the policies or commitment of your campus or city IT department. The OCLC Digital Archive also eliminates the need for your institution to build a costly infrastructure to support your digital collections. For an annual fee for specific services for each collection you can eliminate the need to make huge capital and training investments.

The OCLC Digital Archive reduces the risks associated with long-term storage through commitment to standards. OCLC is one of the active participants in the development of the OAIS standard (Open Archive Information System) which sets the standard for the functions of a digital archive. Commitment to standards is critical in reducing the risk associated with selecting a proprietary system that could become outdated, making your digital collections inaccessible.

Digital and Preservation Resource Centers

OCLC is also establishing Digital and Preservation Resource Centers. We are building on the extensive experience of Preservation Resources, an OCLC division based in Bethlehem, Pennsylvania, that provides digital scanning services and high-quality preservation microfilming for libraries, archives, historical societies and museums. Originally called MAPS (Mid-Atlantic Preservation Service), the organization was established in 1985 to serve the preservation microfilming needs of five Mid-Atlantic research libraries–Columbia University Libraries, Cornell University Library, Princeton University Library, New York State Library and the New York Public Library. It has been a division of OCLC since 1994.

Some of you may know that Preservation Resources scanned and digitized the microfilm of the papers of George Washington, Thomas Jefferson and Abraham Lincoln for the Library of Congress and its American Memory Project.

This month, OCLC will open the OCLC Western Digital & Preservation Resources Center in Lacey, Washington. Like the Bethlehem facility, it will offer training workshops, cooperative project facilitation, and consulting and referral services. And in June, it will start offering reformatting services. The center will serve institutions located in the western United States.

In addition to these three service areas, OCLC is also going to offer Olive software for libraries. Olive is unique technology for turning newspaper microfilm into Web-accessible, article-level searchable newspaper repositories. OCLC is partnering with Olive to help you gain access to the information hidden in your newspaper microfilm archive. Once your newspaper collection has been converted, you can provide users with article-level searchability and collection and page-level browsing.

The launch of these services represents the culmination of a series of research projects and collaborative efforts involving member libraries and OCLC over the past decade. OCLC's pilot program with the U.S. Government Printing Office and other institutions in the Web Document Digital Archive project has helped put in place the infrastructure for the digital archive. I believe it was Deanna Marcum, president of the Council on Library and Information Resources, who said that the greatest challenges in digital archiving are not the technological ones, but the organizational ones. These are questions of who is going to do what, and for how long? At OCLC, we intend to meet the archiving and digital preservation needs of our member libraries by doing what we do best–which is facilitating library cooperation. We will be working closely with our participating libraries in the years ahead to develop digital and preservation services that will indeed stand the test of time.

According to the December 2001 *ARL Bimonthly Report*, ARL libraries spent nearly $100 million on electronic resources in 1999/2000, which was up $23 million from the previous year. That is a hefty increase. Electronic resources now represent 12.9 percent of a library's materials budget. Ten years ago, electronic resources accounted for an estimated 3.6 percent of the materials budget.

Last year at this conference, Paul Gherman proposed a long-term goal for the library that was essentially to close the library and offer all of its services digitally. A concomitant goal was to spend as much as possible of the library budget on information, not infrastructure. Paul, as many of you know, is Director of the Vanderbilt University Library. He is a former member of the OCLC Board of Trustees and is currently a member of the OCLC Members Council. Paul's vision of the digital library may seem a bit extreme at present, but it clearly is focused on the user and not the institution, and on providing digital collections that are much richer and at greater savings than is possible today.

With netLibrary and OCLC, there are new opportunities to shape collection development policy with individual libraries, groups of libraries, and even with publishers. E-book usage is really about access. We now can track usage both inside and outside the library. This new ability to measure usage can help inform collection development. We can determine not only the number of uses of an e-book, but access times, such as peak usage periods. This type of information, while ensuring privacy of individual users, could assist your decision-making. You have the ability to not only develop, but to manage your collection. These tools can also help determine how people actually use information.

With OCLC's initiatives in preservation and archiving, there are new opportunities to bring the special collections of libraries into the Web environment. In this case, collection development is about making what you already own more widely accessible. It is truly development of your existing resources in the best sense of the word.

Clearly, we are making progress toward what Dan Greenstein calls next generation digital libraries.

> . . . the digital library is . . . one star in a much wider constellation . . . known less for the extent and nature of the collections it owns than for the networked information space it defines through a range of online services.[13]

Libraries are on the verge of realizing some long-held dreams about providing access to information to people when and where they want it. With each new advance in selecting, in ordering, in cataloging, in resource sharing, and in reference, we come closer to realizing that shared mutual vision.

Or, as Vannevar Bush said, "There is a new profession of trailblazers, those who delight in the task of establishing useful trails through the enormous mass of the common record."

That profession of trailblazers is in this room, doing important work for research, scholarship and education, not just for today, but for future generations.

NOTES

1. Ketchum-Van Orsdel, L., & Born, K. 1999. "Serials publishing in flux." *Library Journal*, 124(7): p. 48.

2. Manoff, Marlene. 2000. "Hybridity, Mutability, Multiplicity: Theorizing Electronic Library Collections." *Library Trends* (Spring): 860.

3. Rioux, M.A. 1997. "Hunting and Gathering in Cyberspace: Finding and Selecting Web Resources for the Library's Virtual Collection." *Serials Librarian*, 30 (3/4): 129-136

4. Kohl, David. 1997. "Farewell to all that: transforming collection development to fit the virtual library context: The OhioLINK experience," In C.A. Schwarts (Ed.), *Restructuring Academic Libraries: Organizational Development in the Wake of Technological Change*. Chicago: American Library Association: 108-120.

5. Porter, Phil. "10 Years After/A decade of the Web has entangled good and ill," *Columbus Dispatch*, February 18, 2002: 1-H.

6. Okerson, Ann. 2000. "Are We There Yet? Online E-Resources Ten Years After." *Library Trends*: Spring: 685.

7. Berners-Lee, Tim. 1999. *Weaving the Web*. New York: Harper SanFranciso: 123.

8. Berners-Lee, Tim; Hendler, James; and Lassila, Ora. 2001. "The Semantic Web." *Scientific American* (May): 36.

9. Ibid.

10. Brigham, Keith H.; Connaway, Lynn Silipigni; and Lawrence, Stephen. 2001. "Life Cycle Costs of Library Collections: Creation of Effective Performance and Cost Metrics for Library Resources." *College & Research Libraries* (November): 541-553.

11. Ramirez, Diana and Gyeszly, Suzanne. 2000. "netLibrary: a new direction in collection development," *Collection Building*, Vol. 20, Issue 4: 154-164.

12. Kilgour, Frederick G. 1998. *The Evolution of the Book*. New York: Oxford University Press: 152.

13. Greenstein, Daniel. "Next Generation Digital Libraries." VALA 2002 Conference. February 6, 2002. Victorian Library Association.

From the Inside Out:
An Organizational View
of Electronic Resources
and Collection Development

Jennifer A. Younger

SUMMARY. Discusses electronic resources and collection development. Focuses on how e-resources are changing the world of access to information, how and why scholars and research libraries use electronic resources, and how e-resources are to be archived. *[Article copies available for
a fee from The Haworth Document Delivery Service: 1-800-HAWORTH. E-mail address: <getinfo@haworthpressinc.com> Website: <http://www.Haworth Press.com>
© 2002 by The Haworth Press, Inc. All rights reserved.]*

KEYWORDS. Electronic resources, collection development

Good morning and thank you Sul. I am delighted to be taking part in
this conference on electronic resources and collection development in
research libraries. Electronic resources, or ER as we usually say in the
library somehow never mixing them up with the television show, are the
most talked about topic in our world. If this is not true singly, then
surely it is as other topics such as copyright, scholarly publishing, seem
inevitably to lead to electronic resources. Even new books take us there.

Jennifer A. Younger is Director, University Libraries of Notre Dame, Notre Dame,
IN 46556.

This article was presented at the Conference on Electronic Resources and Collection
Development, University of Oklahoma, Oklahoma City, Oklahoma, March 7-8, 2002.

[Haworth co-indexing entry note]: "From the Inside Out: An Organizational View of Electronic Resources and Collection Development." Younger, Jennifer A. Co-published simultaneously in *Journal of Library Administration* (The Haworth Information Press, an imprint of The Haworth Press, Inc.) Vol. 36, No. 3,
2002, pp. 19-38; and: *Electronic Resources and Collection Development* (ed: Sul H. Lee) The Haworth Information Press, an imprint of The Haworth Press, Inc., 2002, pp. 19-38. Single or multiple copies of this article
are available for a fee from The Haworth Document Delivery Service [1-800-HAWORTH, 9:00 a.m. - 5:00
p.m. (EST). E-mail address: getinfo@haworthpressinc.com].

Tom Friedman's book on understanding globalization has deservedly enhanced his reputation as one of America's leading interpreters of world affairs. In his foreword to the Anchor Edition, which is a paperback edition published one year after the hardback edition appeared in April 1999, Tom Friedman comments that, "The new world order is evolving so fast that sometimes I wish this were an electronic book that I could just update every day" (2000, p. x).

The impact of e-resources on libraries has been one of continual change and updating. Since we purchased those first CD-ROMS little more than a decade ago, we have made many changes in our libraries to make them accessible to library users. Those first CD-ROMs were almost book-like in retrospect. They were often indexes kept at the reference desk, supplementary material in books or journals, or stand-alone content in separate packages put on the shelves. Sometimes they were circulated, although more often than not in those early days, use was restricted to the library premises for security and proximity to CD players.

Since then, the inclusion of electronic resources in library collections has grown considerably. One measure is the quadruple growth in spending on e-resources in less than a decade: from 3.6% in 1992-93 to 12.9% in 1999-2000 of the collections budget is now spent on electronic resources, (ARL Supplementary Statistics, 1999-2000, p. 7). This figure is interesting in that it points to steady growth in the purchase of e-resources, yet reveals a continuing dominance of print purchases. Even if we subtract the dollars spent on other formats, such as video or audio, print materials still command a larger share of our collection dollars.

ELECTRONIC IS OVERTAKING PRINT

A funny thing, however, happened on the way to this conference. In reflecting on events and trends in the library, on campus and beyond, I became persuaded that e-resources have already overtaken print resources in their importance to research library collections, though this is not reflected in dollars spent on collections or in volumes held at this moment in time. The promise of e-resources for research library collections in the future are as boundless as those of the printing press were to scholarship and as important to our ability to support learning, teaching and research as the rural electrification program was to the ability of the farmer to increase the productivity and quality of farm life. Before talking about e-resources and collection development, I want to speak briefly about why electronic resources can be said to be overtaking print, because this shift in my thinking sets the stage for my remarks on e-resources and collection development in research libraries.

I was reminded a few weeks ago just how much e-resources are changing the world of access to information. I needed an article that was published in the *Harvard Business Review* in 1994 for which I had the author, title, and all other key information from my search in the *Web of Science*. I gave the information to the senior administrative assistant, who isn't a librarian, with a suggestion she ask the reference librarians for assistance. She said, "Sure, but first I'll look on the Web." This puzzled me, because the *Harvard Business Review* is not a free resource, but I said nothing. She did the search, found the *Harvard Business Review* archive online and learned that she needed only to pay $6 to order an article. In the end, this article was not available because the online archive only went back to 1995 and she got the article the "old fashioned way." She went to the library. This was an interesting event for both of us. She learned what "the library" could offer and I learned again how the Web and e-resources have become a first approach in many instances.

An earlier indicator of the pre-eminence of e-resources appeared in the now ceased Library of Congress periodical *Civilization* in an article by a writer named Daniel Radosh (1999). He started with this question: "What insights can the technology of 1999 deliver about the world as it was a millennium ago?" He researched his essay on the Byzantium entirely on the Internet. His path started with Yahoo! with a search for "year 1000" and "ancient history" which took him to a Web site at the University of Evansville. Along his journey, he visited about 25 Web sites. These sites include "edu" sites, including U of Evansville, Kansas, Carnegie Mellon; "com" sites, including Amazon.com, britannica.com, landsend.com, muslimonline.com; and last, "org" sites, including Corporation for Public Broadcasting and the Center for Millennial Studies.

There is no going back, as was said in "The Wizard of Oz" movie–we're not in Kansas anymore. From simple discussions of e-resources, we're now in the realm of digitization initiatives, digital libraries and digital library services environment where the importance of electronic resources, both those we buy and those we don't buy, has overtaken that of print. Within the library world, we have sought to soothe the fears of those who don't want print to disappear with careful statements recognizing the duality of print and electronic resources for the present and future. Of course, such statements are made not simply to soothe fears, but also because the evidence to date has not suggested printed resources will disappear any time soon, nor will they.

However, the acceleration of activity both in familiar areas, such as journals going online and in new activities, such as preserving digital sources, suggests the pendulum has swung from print to electronic/digital. The future may not have arrived in full reality, but strategically, the future is now defined as electronic. A quick snapshot of activities, though scattered and unsystematic, reveals unmistakably the importance of digital information and, in regard to the topic under discussion at this conference, the ascendance of importance to research library collections and services of electronic resources over print resources.

ELECTRONIC RESOURCES, SCHOLARS AND RESEARCH LIBRARIES

From conversations and studies, we know that scholars in all disciplines are used to and even prefer information that can be accessed from desktops, especially finding aids, catalogs, abstract and indexing services, and online journals. Scholars in all disciplines like and use digitized full-text databases of primary sources, such as Literature Online (Lion), a fully searchable library of more than 330,000 works of English and American fiction, poetry and prose databases published by Chadwyck-Healey (Brockman 2001, 16), as well as library-created digitized collections such as *The Making of America* from the University of Michigan and Cornell University. Though some current digital editions of books online are insufficient for scholarly purposes, lacking proper footnotes or simply not being the appropriate edition, these problems are practical problems resulting from poor choices made in the digitization projects, not indicators that electronic books wouldn't be valued or used. Brockman goes on to say that scholars want broad access to digitally reformatted materials.

Scholars like the ease of access but also the functionality of e-texts. Speaking at the dedication of a renovated library wing at Stanford University of his use of e-texts, President Gerhard Casper said very succinctly: "The electronic medium makes possible, even in areas of traditional humanities scholarship, a thoroughness that was previously unattainable" ([p. 8]). The ease of access is clearly reflected in the use statistics for journals in JSTOR, the national journal storage program currently holding about 150 journal titles in its repository. Kevin Guthrie, president, characterizes JSTOR as a project that has turned a "no-growth industry" into a growth industry. Though my library doesn't have directly comparable use statistics for the off-shelf use of back volumes of journals, the use data from JSTOR is so staggering that it is sensible to accept Kevin's description as accurate (JSTOR News 2002, 4).

At Yale, the librarians have described a role for e-texts in course readings, e.g., putting full chapters on reserves, although they also explicitly recognized that working out issues of copyright could be challenging. There are course readings available electronically for approximately one hundred courses at Notre Dame. Four times as many students are accessing the electronic course readings as are not using e-reserves (Taylor 2002, 8).

A recent study at two small Illinois colleges on the use of e-book devices for course work found positive reactions among students (Peters 2001). Librarians and English faculty used the Franklin ebookman, a PDA-like device, and the RCA REB 1100 in the libraries and English classrooms. Overall, majority of the students judged the handheld portable e-book devices useful. Students were impressed with the imbedded dictionary lookup feature and the ability to underline passages. There were some minuses: screen glare and the lack of pagination, pointing to the need to have a method for quickly and easily finding a specific place in an e-book. Students liked the audio functionality such as playing MP3 files. Faculty found that despite some difficulties such as the lack of pagination, these portable handheld e-book devices did not take away from achieving course objectives and in the future, e-books may even lead toward greater reader persistence.

E-books for reading are but the most recent e-resource to arrive in research library collections to take their place alongside their e-index, e-journal, e-reserves and e-special collection counterparts. Fueled by the success of other e-resources, measured in that elusive statistic known as "hits," the selection of e-books represented a logical progression of events. The readers of e-books, at least at my library, are largely unknown. From time to time, faculty members express great interest in finding or acquiring e-books, but clearly we're still in the beginning stages.

DIGITIZATION INITIATIVES

There is no need to discuss how journal publishing has moved, or is moving, into the digital era. While some journals still remain in only a print medium, the evolutionary path toward e-journals is so clearly established for the future, that the only question is when and how to go digital for scholarly journals. A multiplicity of new digitization initiatives are focusing on library special collections encompassing a wide range of primary sources, images, texts, and sound, and full texts on microfilm and paper, of which several projects are among the most well known, American Memory, Making of America. New companies are creating e-books from university press back lists. In light of this activity, a recent report from the Council on Library and Information Resources states "there is every reason to believe that within a decade, significant corpora of texts will be available for use from the desktop in a number of fields" (Nichols, p. 27).

Established scholars are being encouraged to write "born digital" e-books, the front lists now distributed in paper. With a $3 million grant from The Andrew W. Mellon Foundation, the American Council of Learned Societies (ACLS) is sponsoring an electronic publishing initiative for scholarly monographs in history (http://www.historyebook.org/). Though ACLS is not suggesting the list of new scholarly monographs in print feature will disappear from the *Chronicle of Higher Education*, ACLS is promoting the more rapid development of electronic publication for book-length works of high quality and accelerating the involvement of its member societies in the evolution of electronic scholarly communications. In its view, there is no escaping the fact that technology has moved us into "a transition from a print-based world to an era in which scholarly discourse will be conducted largely within a globally networked electronic environment." As supporting evidence, ACLS points to the current reviews of electronic projects in journals and *The New York Times*. The History E-Book Project will take this further not only by implementing such reviews, but is initiating discussions with The American Historical Review with the American Association for History and Computing to set standards for compiling and reviewing history e-books. This represents the next phase making back lists of titles available electronically is a more or less straightforward process of converting and coding the text. This project will address the questions of concern to scholars–how e-books are written, submitted, reviewed and considered in the tenure process.

Further encouragement for scholarly writers to "go digital" comes from the Knight Higher Education Collaborative. *Op. Cit.* 9 from the Knight Higher Education Collaborative crossed my desk, yes, admittedly on paper, though the publication is also online. Its purpose is to promote digital publications in the humanities and social sciences. The essay addresses several concerns, one of which is how individual contributions to knowledge can be broadly accessible, a reaffirming of the voice of the humanities and social sciences just as the practical advances in science and other fields are valued. In considering how the voice of the humanities and social sciences can more effectively reach out to the public, the essay concludes, "We believe an important component of this process is an inventive exploration of the possibilities of digital publication both as an augmentation to and at time a substitute for print publication" (10).

Nationally and internationally, scholars in training have new opportunities for publishing in digital formats. In the United States, the Networked Digital Library of Theses and Dissertations (NDLTD) (http://www.ndltd.org/) has multiple goals worth noting: (1) "to improve graduate education by allowing students to produce electronic documents, use digital libraries, and understand issues in publishing," (2) "to empower students to convey a richer message through the use of multimedia and hypermedia technologies," and (3) "to empower universities to unlock their information resources." NDLTD has 138 members: 122 member universities (including 3 consortia) and 16 other institutions, including some prestigious institutions such as Cal Tech, MIT and Vanderbilt. Electronic dissertations are internationally supported by UNESCO (http://www.eduserver.de/unesco/). UNESCO is examining the possibilities of formulating an international strategy for creating and disseminating electronic theses and dissertations (ETDs). In September 1999, UNESCO headquarters invited a number of international experts to review existing electronic theses and dissertations (ETD) projects, to define the needs of developing countries in this area and to discuss possible international action. Of course, dissertations aren't fully developed scholarship nor are they books. They are, however, a training ground for the next generation of scholars. Basic activities, including Electronic dissertations, are picking up speed, training new generations of scholars in this new mode of publishing.

With the Web, everyone is a publisher. We often think first individuals in this regard, but organizations and corporations such as the Association of Research Libraries and Fidelity Investments have made "gray literature" broadly accessible with a few key strokes. The proceedings of membership meetings, the bimonthly report, statistics and other occasional publications from the Association of Research Libraries are accessible online. Potential investors can find company information, shareholder reports and investment advice online at the Fidelity Investments Web site. Within the collection development arena, if there was any doubt about the significance of freely available e-resources, the recently published guidelines by Lou Pitschmann in the recent CLIR publication titled *Building sustainable collections of free third-party web based resources* point to the reality of including these information resources in our "collections."

KNOWLEDGE AND LEARNING IN THE ERA OF THE WEB

Technologists are more aware of their users and are moving toward developing systems that are more "user friendly." Usability is the buzzword for future developments. Dr. Eric Shaffer, a psychologist who specializes in technology and human interaction, spoke about this last year at the Internet Librarian conference. He postulated that the 1980s were about hardware, the 1990s about software, and the next wave of technology will be about usability (Shaffer 2001). If we want the population to be able to do more than surf and read e-mail, the more complex web applications will have to become more user friendly. Within research libraries, we too are conducting usability studies of our Web sites to determine what makes a site easy and productive to use. There are activities now that many of us find easier to do manually, such as browsing through a shelf of books or journals. In part this is because we are accustomed to doing so, but also in part because the print formats still support browsing and paging forward and backward more easily than do the electronic formats. On the other hand, the ability in the electronic environment to go directly from a citation in one source to the full text in another source without moving from one's chair, and back again to find another citation and text is functionality not possible in the print environment.

In 1999, Robert Darnton envisioned a new kind of book, an electronic book with layers in a pyramid (Darnton 1999). Each layer would have a different purpose, a concise account, expanded versions of different aspects of the argument, different kinds of documentation with interpretative essays, and even a layer with suggestions for teaching. Naturally, people might read differently, pursuing linearly or not as they were interested in following the texts. In his new kind of book, the various texts could be printed and bound, but according to the specifications of the reader. Computer screens would take advantage of the searching functionality, although he predicted that reading would still be from paper.

Since then, there is a growing belief that the knowledge media, a term bringing together computing, telecommunication and cognitive sciences, will change the relationship people have with knowledge. The knowledge media define the technical aspects first of transferring the content from one medium to another, and then to redefining how the knowledge is presented and used. Interactivity online is different than the interactions that took place between readers and printed texts. The World Wide Web will prove to be a transformative medium, as important as electricity, and the current gradual development is accelerating in pace and impact (Brown 2000). Unlike most media, the Web is a two-way, push and pull, medium. It draws the inquirer into its databases, responds, and then responds again when the question is rephrased. The Web supports multiple expressions of thought, integrating and showcasing textual, visual, and audio expressions, not unlike what we see in films, but when interactivity is added, there is a new dimension in our learning. And where multiple expressions of thought are included in an e-book, printing on paper will not capture the wholeness of the book. Darnton too anticipates the development of learning in ways we cannot imagine today and the development of electronic books as "a tool for prying problems apart and opening up a new space for the extension of learning."

Discovery based learning will gain preeminence as Web surfing fuses learning and entertainment. Kids go for action when confronted with a new system. They get on the Web and link, lurk, and watch how others are doing things, and then try. This is the loop in which navigation, discovery and judgment all come into play in situ. The focus shifts toward learning in situ with and from each other. Learning becomes situated in action; social and cognitive, concrete rather than abstract, intertwined with judgment and exploration. The Web becomes not only an informational and social resources tool but also a learning medium. Learning becomes a part of action and knowledge creation (Brown 2000).

New generations of readers are in the making. At Xerox's Palo Alto Research Center, researchers gave teenagers the opportunity to design their school of the future, observing their thoughts and results (Brown 2000, 3). The researchers believe that discovery-based learning will gain pre-eminence over what we experienced as "authority-based, lecture-oriented" learning. E-books will certainly be a part of this environment though it is very likely new readers and writers will have changed our concept of e-books to something we don't have today.

The population of those able to use e-resources is increasing rapidly. A news item reported in the *Wall Street Journal* highlighted the expanding use of the Internet in the United States. New numbers from the U.S. Commerce Department (2002) showed that the number of Americans who use the Web passed the 50% mark for the first time last year. One hundred forty three million Americans, or 54% of the population, were using the Internet as of September 2001, reflecting a substantial increase from the previous year. The most heavily used activity remains e-mail, which is regularly used by 45% of the population. Though the increase here is modest, from 35% in 2000, the increase suggests a steadiness likely to result in a continuing increase next year. This is especially likely when viewed in context of the figures for kids and teenagers under the age of 17, where 90% are using computers. Growth in Internet use is rising faster among those with the lowest incomes, under $15,000 annually, than it is by households with the highest incomes. The "digital divide" may be lessening though there may still be cause for concern depending on whether the Internet access is from homes, schools or work.

The implications of these activities in learning and Web use seem clear. People's expectations for what they can do online are changing rapidly and are being shaped by their experiences in everyday life: buying books at Amazon.com, paying bills online through their bank, seeing and hearing the latest news on the CNN Website. A single example–consulting an online dictionary in preference to a "regular" dictionary summarizes the important symbolic transition many people have already made to a world where "it's the Web" has become the mantra. As we can observe, the people who use libraries are advancing in their use of computers and the Web on many dimensions. At the Digital Library Federation Fall Forum last year, Barbara Taranto of the New York Public Library, identified the evolving skills of our audiences as a primary factor in why libraries must move forward in understanding how digital resources can and will be used.

ELECTRONIC RESOURCES ARE MORE IMPORTANT THAN PRINT RESOURCES TO RESEARCH LIBRARIES

Information and knowledge resources are going digital in steadily increasing numbers. At some point in the future, they will outnumber print resources and it will be observed that electronic resources are more important than print resources to research library collections. My premise today is that, even before this quantitative shift happens, the relative importance of print and electronic resources has already shifted in favor of electronic resources. Importance is a value judgement that describes the superior value or worth of something in relation to other things. I do not dispute that print resources are, and will remain, important for the foreseeable future. It is my observation, however, that as measured by the focus of our energy, time and talents on the design, use and most recently, the preservation of electronic resources, they are already more important for the future of scholarship and research library collection than are print resources. In recognizing and adopting this perspective, we as librarians can take steps to ensure more reliable and useful development and use of electronic resources.

It is only a matter of time, a short time in my view, before electronic resources overtake print resources in current publishing and preferred mode of use. On the measure of absolute numbers of all volumes past, present and future, print resources may retain their numerical dominance for some number of years to come, but not their dominance in importance to scholarly activities. In describing our vision of the University Libraries of Notre Dame as a great destination for learning and research, I put it this way to the college deans. Go Irish! Go Digital!

E-RESOURCES AND COLLECTION MANAGEMENT

Turning now to e-resources and collection development, the subject of this conference, it is obvious to everyone here that electronic resources introduce new complexities and opportunities into collection development. Your own work as well as the literature attest to that. As mentioned, my assumption is that e-resources have overtaken print resources in importance for the future despite the fact that we currently spend more dollars on buying print than we do for e-resources, and my remarks reflect that assumption. I draw as well on activities already underway in libraries and my perspective as the director of a medium sized research library, that like your libraries, is both driving and responding to the new complexities and opportunities brought about by e-resources. I will speak to two points. First, that as we move toward greater reliance on electronic resources in library collections, the issue is archiving, not patron use. Second, that because e-resources are more easily delivered on-demand than are print, there is new potential for greater differentiation between building collections and meeting user information needs.

Two years ago, in speaking with college deans at the University of Notre Dame, I described the significant challenge faced by the library in regard to building collections and meeting faculty information needs. Superinflation in the costs of library materials, new curricular or research programs, cross-disciplinary programs and the desire for academic excellence at the university have together put enormous pressure on the library collections budget at Notre Dame as they have at most research libraries. I identified thirteen strategies for addressing this challenge, all familiar to this audience, and strategies such as consortial licensing which has been in use for a number of years. Two strategies, however, are of special interest today because they speak to the role of electronic resources in our collections and because they suggest a new duality in our thinking about collection development and meeting information needs. The first strategy is to cancel paper subscriptions to titles where we currently are receiving the title in both paper and electronic format. The second strategy is to cancel journals used infrequently and purchase articles on demand.

ARCHIVING OF ELECTRONIC RESOURCES IS THE ISSUE

At Notre Dame, we are in the process of reviewing serial subscriptions and exploring the feasibility of canceling the paper version in favor of the electronic version. There are of course questions to be asked and answered. It is clear that even in collections where over fifty percent of the current subscriptions are in electronic format, it is still not a simple matter to cancel the paper. What is most interesting, though, as we move toward greater reliance on electronic resources, is that use is not the issue. Our faculty did not question accessing serials in their electronic format. Instead they pointed to the need for adequate and affordable printing for students, for which we are and will continue to make local provisions in the same way we have met patron needs for making copies of printed text. Second, they asked how does the library assure these e-resources will be permanently archived and preserved for future generations. Even though we have contracts for "access in perpetuity," we don't own any physical volumes on either paper or an electronic medium, and the question of how we can guarantee archiving for something we don't own is a question that must be addressed.

Research libraries do not have the luxury of avoiding the question of archiving and preservation of resources as this is part of our mission. Digital archiving is also not a problem that Notre Dame can independently solve nor has it been completely solved in the national arena. There are permanent repositories such as JSTOR, but to date, these electronic repositories include a very small percent of materials to be archived. Accordingly, my answer to the faculty begins with the sense expressed a year ago by Martin Runkle, University of Chicago, that activities such as JSTOR, which creates a reliable and secure scholarly archive, cannot go away (Runkle 2002). In thinking about his observation, I expanded on it to mean that digital archiving and preservation of electronic resources will happen because it is unimaginable that it will not take place. Therefore, we can cancel subscriptions to print resources in favor of subscriptions to electronic resources.

Fortunately, there is work in progress that supports this imagined future. In 1999, a group of librarians and publishers deliberated on requirements and responsibilities for archiving electronic scholarly journals so as to be able to guarantee access in one hundred years (*Preservation of Electronic Scholarly Journals* 2002). Their work resulted in criteria that outline how a repository must act (*Minimum criteria for an archival repository of digital scholarly journals 2000*). The criteria begin with the need to be a "trusted party" which is achieved through conforming to the minimum criteria, both as initially defined and presumably as criteria might evolve. A repository must define its mission in the context of the needs of research libraries and scholarly publishers; it must negotiate and accept deposits, and then make that information available according to the terms negotiated with the publisher. Most importantly, the criteria call for a network approach to ensure appropriate redundancy of archived contents.

On the basis of the consensus achieved among librarians, publishers and others consulted, the Mellon Foundation has funded seven projects on archiving e-journals from research libraries in the northeast and on the west coast. Each project addresses a specific aspect of archiving. With Elsevier, the project at Yale is sorting out questions of discrete responsibilities, starting with those of the responsibilities of the publisher to ensure day-to-day access, what happens when a publisher goes out of business and how to provide for long term traditional archival needs (*Proposal for a digital preservation 2002*). The project will develop a detailed archival plan and computing test-bed for the second and third circumstances. In the future, research libraries such as Notre Dame, will be able to subscribe to these archives of the future much as we now subscribe to JSTOR.

In the digital world, planning for data archiving and repository services for scholarly information in digital information is economically and technically complex (Ekman 2000). The formats in which scholarly information is disseminated will go beyond the traditional formats of books or journals to include Web sites where publishers, owners, originators and keepers may have contributed to the site.

While publishers and/or creators own the intellectual property, traditionally it is libraries that have archived it. Future data archiving will likely involve many players requiring new partnership among publishers, learned societies, telecommunications companies, libraries and universities.

Successful data archiving for responding to future scholarly inquires also requires a national preservation plan. Last year (2001), Congress awarded $100 million to the Library of Congress (LC) to pursue the archiving and preservation of digital materials. On behalf of the LC, the Council of Library and Information Resources (CLIR) is coordinating the first steps of collecting and synthesizing information from content creators, distributors and users that can then serve as the basis for developing a national strategy for the preservation of digital materials. Four categories of common interests emerged from their papers and meetings: technical and architectural infrastructure, economic and legal issues, collection development, and societal and institutional issues. Further, there was broad agreement that the ultimate long-term preservation strategy will require a distributed system under which commercial, nonprofit and government agencies will work in collaboration with the Library of Congress, research libraries, archives, museums, and other institutions (Marcum 2002).

The development of a national preservation set of strategies will accomplish two important goals. It will support the ability of research libraries to manage access to e-resources separately from the permanent archiving and preservation of those e-resources. Decoupling digital archiving and digital access will safely allow libraries such as Notre Dame to purchase access only to the electronic formats. Knowledgeable individuals are raising questions about how electronic repositories will be funded when access is separated from ownership (Guthrie 2001). This seems not only likely, but desirable to avoid excessive redundancy in digital archiving; perhaps the preservation budgets will expand to pay for subscriptions to digital archiving. Second, it will support the ability of research libraries to develop some local collections with a goal in mind of meeting information needs instead of building comprehensive collections. To the extent that some research libraries find this useful in meeting local information needs, a national plan for archiving will ensure that e-resources not in local collections are archived regionally or nationally.

THE POTENTIAL FOR GREATER DIFFERENTIATION BETWEEN BUILDING COLLECTIONS AND MEETING USER INFORMATION NEEDS

That brings me to the second issue. In research libraries, collections are the *sina qua non* of our existence. We place the highest value on building library collections as the primary means by which we meet the information needs of faculty and students. We call it collection development, not meeting information needs, because the goal is to build a collection that will stand the test of time for meeting present and future information needs. Collection development policies articulate collection goals of coherence, balance, and comprehensiveness and determine what materials should be selected. The library collection is the heart of our ability to meet campus information needs and is the preferred tool of most students and faculty.

Not only do our collections meet user information needs, but they also preserve recorded knowledge of the ages. In the words of President Casper at the rededication of a wing of Stanford Library, "The holdings of the university library, paper, object, and digital, are one of the means by which the university performs its role as the custodian of that rational process" (Casper, 2000, 13). We build comprehensive collections for that purpose and have in the past been judged by the quality of these collections. This value system is shared by all: university presidents, librarians and faculty. The library is a laboratory and university faculty want the collection to "have it all," and to be close at hand for immediate access. If a book or journal isn't in the library collection, there is a perception that the collection, or the library, has failed. Again, this is often a perception shared by faculty and collection development librarians.

This value system is not the only set of foundational values. Special libraries without extensive collections are the basis of the "special library service model" where the primary performance criteria is not the development of a collection but rather meeting the information needs of individual users through local or other resources. According to a new librarian who came to Notre Dame from a reference and information center in a large accounting firm, the goal did not lie in developing a fine collection. What mattered was whether the relevant materials could be obtained on a timely basis without regard to whether the materials came from the collection or from a document delivery service. If we in research libraries greatly expand use of a strategy that relies on more on-demand purchasing of journal articles instead of subscriptions, we will have to expand our values to put as high a value on meeting information needs as we do on building collections.

Acquiring materials on demand is not a new strategy. Collection development policies often acknowledge the need to obtain resources from outside the collection with mention of other sources, such as the Center for Research Libraries or interlibrary loan services. Driven by escalating costs, some research libraries have adopted a different position in appropriating dollars for collection development and on demand document delivery. At the University of Illinois Urbana-Champaign (UIUC) Tina Chrzastowski and Brian Olesko reduced journal subscriptions to stay within the limits of the collection budget and in lieu of subscriptions to all journals, incorporated more use of on demand document delivery to meet information needs (1997). The UIUC Chemistry Library continues to have a collection but with a different purpose. The purpose of the collection is no longer to own and preserve all of the extant chemistry literature but rather to work concurrently with document delivery to meet the information needs of faculty. The UIUC Chemistry Library is putting into operation the idea of collecting for use expressed a decade ago by the director of another research library who noted that demand-driven service prototypes needed to be created because having only a single model, the warehouse model, of a research library is not viable (Shaughnessy 1991).

The ideal, however, of a comprehensive or at the least, a research level, collection on-site is embedded in our heritage and it is human nature to want to do what is most valued. If libraries such as Notre Dame are to be successful in making cost-effective use of on-demand delivery of journal articles or books instead of purchasing these materials, we have to ensure these activities are fully acknowledged in our values. Collections and document delivery services must both be highly valued as a means of meeting information needs.

This also means a careful setting of library and institutional priorities for differentiation between the equally worthy goals of building collections of distinction for the global scholarly community or meeting the information needs of the campus scholarly community. Whether the values are changing is a matter for discussion, but the annual statistics collected by the Association of Research Libraries show that "no matter what the underlying causal relations, research libraries are exchanging some of the traditional archival imperatives for the user demands of information here and now" (Association of Research Libraries 2001, 10). Clearly electronic resources bring new opportunities for the service model. Some research libraries have purchased specified amounts of journal use in a database instead of subscribing to titles. Similarly, netLibrary has offered the opportunity to purchase a specific number of e-books with the selection of specific titles to be made by users as they find titles they need instead of by librarians as they anticipate what titles will be needed. A fundamental change in collection development is in the making as the "function of selection moves more and more into the hands of users who will exploit the tools provided by libraries and others to identify and retrieve material through the network" (Shreeves 1997, 386).

Research libraries will not abandon their role as the repositories of knowledge though individual libraries may well adopt an approach that brings together under one roof the differentiated collection goals of "just-in-case" and "just-in-time" (Gherman and Schmidt 2001). Research libraries collectively, not individually, will preserve all knowledge for future generations. Assuming that to be inevitable, we must also acknowledge that this perspective may well call for a greater financial collaboration and support in the preservation of knowledge.

Where the intent of collection development in any specific subject in any individual library changes to focus on acquiring resources, either to become part of a collection or to be given to a user to meet their information need, the job responsibilities of collection development librarians will broaden to include reference as well as collection development activities. Reference services define their service goals in terms of users, individuals as well as groups who share common characteristics, such as undergraduate or graduate students, whose needs can be anticipated only to a general degree. "Collection development" librarians will assess how to meet user needs and determine the most appropriate role for the library collections and reference services. "Collection development" librarians will maintain close contact with faculty for purposes beyond getting recommendations for new purchases for the collections, informing faculty of how their needs can be met through a wide range of library services. Much of our future relevance will be derived from services provided, especially those services that find and organize access to information resources with no regard for whether they are owned or delivered by the library. The primary performance criterion for research libraries will expand accordingly to include both collection and reference services because meeting information needs of users is a collaboration between collection development and reference functions.

CLOSING REMARKS

Electronic resources have overtaken print resources in their importance to research library collections. Though the statistics reveal that research libraries still spend more dollars on buying print resources than on electronic resources, this will shift dramatically very soon as more research libraries drop print subscriptions in favor of electronic, and the expenditures are fully recorded in the electronic resources column. The future may not have arrived in full reality, but the stage is being set through the work of many parties in resolving the major issue of digital archiving and preservation. Strategically, the future is now defined as electronic.

There has never been a better time to be a librarian. We have our work cut out for us as we move forward in collecting and preserving the knowledge of the ages for all time, yet we have more opportunities for doing so than ever before. It seems at times that we have been outbranded by the Web. Our image is one of a place for books. We are sometimes overshadowed by the ease with which people can find information on the Web though over the years we have been successful in creating strong bonds between libraries and library users. Our collections serve as scholarly laboratories and we will not abandon that role. We are rapidly incorporating e-resources into our collections and services, shaping and reshaping the ways in which we carry out our mission of preserving knowledge and meeting the information needs of our constituencies. It is rewarding to be taking part in a conference where complacency is not the name of the game.

SELECTED REFERENCES

Association of Research Libraries. *ARL Statistics 1999-2000*. Washington, DC: ARL, 2001. 129 pp.

Brockman, William S., Laura Neumann, Carole L. Palmer, and Tonyia J. Tidline. *Scholarly work in the Humanities and the Evolving Information Environment*. Washington, DC: Digital Library Federation and Council on Library and Information Resources, December 2001. *http://www.clir.org/pubs/reports/pub104/pub104.pdf*.

Brown, John Seely. 2000. "Growing up digital: How the Web changes work, education and the ways people learn." *Change* 32: issue 2: 11 p (March/April).

Casper, Gerhard. *Who Needs a Library Anyway? Remarks on the Opening of the Bing Wing of the Cecil H. Green Library, 12 October 1999*. Stanford University Libraries, 2000. [14 pp.].

Chrzastowski, Tina and Brian M. Olesko. "Chemistry Journal Use and Cost: A Longitudinal Study. *Library Resources & Technical Services* 41(2): 101-111 (April 1997).

Darnton, Robert. *The New Age of the Book*. The New York Review of Books March 18, 1999. *http://www.nybooks.com/articles/546* Accessed 3-18-02.

Digital Library Federation. *Minimum criteria for an archival repository of digital scholarly journals*: Version 1.2, May 15, 2000. *http://www.diglib.org/preserve/criteria.htm* Accessed 3-18-02.

Ekman, Richard. H. 2000. "Can Libraries of digital materials last forever? *Change* 32, 2: 22-29 (Mar/Apr2000).

Epstein, Jason. *Reading: The Digital Future*. The New York Review of Books July 5, 2001 *http://www.nybooks.com/articles/14318* Accessed 3-19-02.

Friedman, Thomas L. *2000. The Lexus and the Olive Tree*. New York: Anchor Books, *2000*.

Gherman, Lisa B. and Schmidt, Karen A. "Finding the right balance: campus involvement in the collections allocation process." *Library Collections, Acquisitions, & Technical Services* 25:421-433 (2001).

Guthrie, Kevin. "Archiving in the Digital Age." *EDUCAUSE Review* 36,6: 56-64 (November/December 2001).

JSTOR Usage. *JSTOR News* 6, 1: (March 2002). Accessible at *http://www.jstor.org/news/index.html.*

Marcum, Deanna B. *A National Plan for Digital Preservation: What Does it Mean for the Library Community?* CLIR Issues: Number 25 January/February 2002. *http://www. clir.org/pubs/issues/issues25.html* Accessed 3-18-02.

Minimum criteria for an archival repository of digital scholarly journals. Version 1.2, May 15, 2000. Digital Library Federation. Accessed 3-18-2002 at *http://www.diglib. org/preserve/criteria.htm.*

Nichols, Stephen G. and Abby Smith. *The Evidence in Hand: Report of the Task Force on the Artifact in Library Collections*. Washington, DC: Council on Library and Information Resources, November 2001. *http://www.clir.org/pubs/reports/pub103/contents. html.*

Op.Cit. Policy Perspectives, vol. 10, number 3, December 2001. Knight Higher Education Collaborative; University of Pennsylvania, 2001. *http://www.irhe.upenn.edu/pubs.*

Peters, Thomas A., compiler. *Academic Libraries Take an E-Look at E-Books: Spoon River College and Eureka College, November 30, 2001*. Thomas Peters, Project Evaluator: Director, Center for Library Initiatives, Committee on Institutional Cooperation, 2001. Accessed 3-18-02 at *http://www.geocities.com/lbell927/eBkFinal.*

Pitschmann, Louis A. *Building Sustainable collections of Free Third-Party Web Resources*. Washington, DC: Digital Library Federation and Council on Library and Information Resources, June 2001. 44 pages.

Preservation of electronic scholarly journals. Digital Library Federation. *http://www. diglib.org/preserve/presjour.htm* Accessed 3-18-02.

Proposal for a digital preservation collaboration between The Yale University Library and Elsevier Science, 10 October 2000. http://www.diglib.org/preserve/yaleprop.htm Accessed 3-20-02.

Radosh, Daniel. "The Y1K Problem." *Civilization:* 92-95 (October/November 1999).

Runkle, Martin. Telephone call with the author on March 19, 2002.

Shaffer, Eric. "Library Science and Usability Engineering." Paper presented November 7, 2001 at the Internet Librarian 2001 Conference, Pasadena, CA. November 6-8, 2001.

Shaughnessy, Thomas W. "From Ownership to Access: A Dilemma for Library Managers." *Journal of Library Administration* 14: 1-7 (1991).

Shreeves, Edward. 1997. "Is there a future for cooperative collection development in the digital age?" *Library Trends* 45 (3): 373-390.

Taranto, Barbara. ET call home. *Who's out there: The issue of audience in the digital age*. Paper presented at the Digital Library Federation Fall Forum, November 17, 2001, Pittsburgh, PA.

Taylor, Clara. 2002. "Electronic reserves update." *Access: News from the University Libraries of Notre Dame* 80: 8-9 (Spring 2002).

United States. Department of Commerce. *A Nation Online: How Americans are Expanding their use of the Internet*. Washington, DC: National Telecommunications and Information Administration, 2002. Accessed 3-18-2002 at *http://www.ntia.doc.gov/ntiahome/dn/*.

What Administrators Talk About When They Talk About Libraries

Barbara McFadden Allen

SUMMARY. The author gives personal suggestions about ways in which librarians might think about their own work and role in leading their library toward the new hybrid of print and digital collections and services. *[Article copies available for a fee from The Haworth Document Delivery Service: 1-800-HAWORTH. E-mail address: <getinfo@haworthpressinc.com> Website: <http://www.HaworthPress.com> © 2002 by The Haworth Press, Inc. All rights reserved.]*

KEYWORDS. Committee on Institutional Cooperation (CIC), traditional vs. electronic collections

For the past three years, I have had the pleasure of working with and for the senior administrators of the twelve CIC member universities (the eleven members of the Big Ten Athletic Conference and the University of Chicago). Prior to accepting this position as Director of this consortium, I served to lead and direct the program of library collaboration for the CIC known as the CIC Center for Library Initiatives.

While libraries are the jewel in the crown of our collaborations, we have collaborative programs and research projects across the entire spectrum–from sharing study abroad and less commonly taught language offerings across our institutions; to multimillion dollar annual purchases of scientific supplies, to entirely new programs of instruction and research such as our newly formed American Indian Studies Consortium, the CIC has a 42 year history of deep collaboration.

Barbara McFadden Allen is Director of the Committee on Institutional Cooperation (CIC).

[Haworth co-indexing entry note]: "What Administrators Talk About When They Talk About Libraries." Allen, Barbara McFadden. Co-published simultaneously in *Journal of Library Administration* (The Haworth Information Press, an imprint of The Haworth Press, Inc.) Vol. 36, No. 3, 2002, pp. 39-44; and: *Electronic Resources and Collection Development* (ed: Sul H. Lee) The Haworth Information Press, an imprint of The Haworth Press, Inc., 2002, pp. 39-44. Single or multiple copies of this article are available for a fee from The Haworth Document Delivery Service [1-800-HAWORTH, 9:00 a.m. - 5:00 p.m. (EST). E-mail address: getinfo@haworthpressinc.com].

I'm going to summarize my conversations with a variety of senior administrators in our member universities, talk about why those impressions are important to your success and that of your libraries, and offer some suggestions about ways in which you might think about your own work and your role in leading the library toward the new hybrid of print and digital collections and services. In my opinion, the most successful libraries will lead this change through a combination of stakeholder education and influence building, careful management and stewardship of existing staff and resources, and astutely capturing every available resource to focus attention on the future and moving forward into the future while protecting areas of excellence in the "traditional" or print-based collections.

As you've doubtless guessed, my observations come from the research university perspective, but I believe are relevant for those working in any academic environment, and while the thoughts of administrators in the public, special, or school library setting may differ, I believe those of you from outside the academy will gain some value from these remarks, as well. Particularly if you think about administrators as those who, ultimately, influence your finances and who can support or abandon you through challenging and difficult times–not unlike a board in a public institution. Also, I hasten to point out that most of my observations and recommendations are just that–my own observations and that of others gathered by and large through informal means. Nevertheless, I believe these observations to be valid when considering how effective we are, and in thinking about ways in which we could improve our libraries and the services we provide. That digital and electronic information resources and services greatly improve access to information is a given in my remarks. Others here will speak on the specifics of these benefits. I will start from the assumption that we will need to collect and manage both traditional and electronic collections.

I recently posed four questions to administrators in the CIC member universities, polling 12 research vice presidents, 12 deans, and 12 provosts. I received 13 responses, and there results were as follows:

Thinking about research libraries in general, please "grade" libraries on their application of new computer and information technologies to improve and transform various library functions:

	Deans(3)	VPs(4)	Provosts(6)
Enhancing access to digital information	B	A	A-
Providing enhanced research tools	B	A-	B+

Enhancing access to traditional collections	B+	C+	B
Improving customer service	B	B+	B+

I should also point out that in their responses, administrators almost universally noted the challenges to libraries presented by increasing prices for print and digital publications, the need to juggle expectations of users to provide both, and the great strides libraries have made in successfully adopting new technology. Most interesting to me, and relevant to my discussion today, is that the one mildly negative comment I heard from a provost was, "While I know libraries have made progress in all these areas, especially in digital access, I'm not hearing positive feedback from my faculty, which tells me that they do not share my high opinion"–an instance when there may be a lack of communication between the library and the faculty.

In other conversations provosts have had about libraries, I can tell you that:

- They support out libraries' efforts to expand access to collections through cooperative collection management;
- They believe we should aggressively expand our collections to include digital resources;
- They understand the dynamics of the scholarly communication chain and the underlying economics and are willing to contribute to those discussions (here, in fact, the provosts of the Big XII and the Greater Western Library Alliance have also been leaders);
- They encourage us to change our old models of comparative data on our collections as increasingly meaningless; and
- They see our libraries as leaders in identifying entirely new models of publishing for our research universities–so much so that in our universities the provosts have invested in a pilot project to create a new electronic publishing partnership between our libraries and presses.

Let me draw from another example. In 1999, I conducted a modest study, along with Chandra Prahba of OCLC to gauge faculty response and satisfaction with our CIC Virtual Electronic Library (allowing patrons unmediated access and interlibrary loan to the library catalogs of our member universities). The most amazing finding, was that no matter how hard we make it for patrons to find information on the web and through our catalogs, they consistently perceive that their service was faster and better than the "old" methods of access, ILL, and delivery. Whether they were retrieving digital or print materials, and whether or not the items were held in their home library–those we interviewed perceived they had access to more information than was available in their library alone, and perceived that they had faster access to those materials–apparently owing to the fact that the user felt they controlled the process.

Now, let me jump from the realm of the leaders, faculty, and library users in our universities, and travel to the realm of the public sector and those who hold the increasingly smaller purse strings of our universities: the state legislators. I was recently at a meeting of state government leaders from a number of Midwestern states. These included, usually, the chairs of the house and senate budget committees for higher education, the head of the states higher education board, and a smattering of employees from the offices of the governors or other state officials. The meeting kicked off with a very provocative and erudite oration from the President of a large, public research university. As an ice-breaker and audience interaction exercise, the speaker asked the group to consider the following question: What is the single greatest waste of resources on our campuses? The answer the speaker was seeking was "our students time." But, to my great shock, the audible response from the audience was "the library." Followed by much grumbling about the exorbitant prices of electronic information sources and a perceived lack of good resource management.

What are the key themes emerging from these responses? From the administrative and faculty side within the CIC members universities:

- Recognition of the centrality of the library to the mission of the research university
- A very positive perception about the ability of the library to transform service and collections through the application of digital technologies
- Trust in the ability of the library to provide stewardship of the collections
- An encouragement to pursue collaboration as a strategy for increasing access to information and collections
- Recognition and acceptance of the role of collaboration in delivering services
- And, of course, this is wholly unscientific and anecdotal, and those who did not respond may not share these feelings, and those who did respond may simply not realize things could be any better.

From the anecdote about the state meeting, I believe what we are seeing is symptomatic of the uninformed and uninvolved. I believe that 5 years ago, some of those same university administrators I spoke with might actually have answered the same way. Our library leaders have done a terrific job of leading and influencing decision making about and support for libraries.

The perception of a strong library yields benefits in political support, which I posit translates into financial support (ultimately). Administrators who understand the library support the library: those who are ignorant do not.

Let's look at what this means for you. Our librarians face enormous challenges in providing stewardship to some of the greatest print-based collections in the world. They face staggering costs for journals, and increasing pressures to provide digital services and collections–though no one is willing to give up their print access. Others here will recite the horror stories about how large your collection budgets would have to be to buy everything in every format and provide access to it all.

There are a number of strategies that might be used to transition to this hybrid print/digital future, to develop and promote entirely new services of which we've not yet even conceived, and protect and provide access to our print resources.

The collection manager stands in what many consider an unenviable position: with this vision of the hybrid collection shining like a beacon on one side, and the realities of the budget, the old guard faculty and suspicious staff members on the other. I well know how disheartening it can be to push for change in the collection budget and with the staff and faculty, only to have someone in upper administration fold on the issue at hand.

Unfortunately (or fortunately) that is the job of the collection manager. If we needed only someone to manage the budget, we would hire accountants. If the bibliographers and subject specialists and faculty all worked together amazingly well and resources were unlimited, there would be no need for you to work with them and lead them to new visions of the library.

Leadership and influence building are your jobs! You must understand and embrace this role. Specialists (be they faculty or bibliographers) exist to specialize and they are going to fight fiercely to protect their turf–and that is the nature of their job. Your role is to blend these disparate interests, maintain momentum for areas of investment in programs and collections of excellence, while also leading toward the future. In such a strategy one might:

- Maintain and protect existing areas of excellence in the collection and services
- Devote every new dollar to target areas of strategic focus
- Blend the interests of many into a cohesive, simple message and tell that story over and over and over again–supporting a move to new and better vision through influence building
- Recognize, champion, celebrate all of the successes
- Interact constantly with all stakeholders–human interaction is essential.

In the end, it is about where you focus your attention. Assuming that you have outstanding management skills including personnel and fiscal management and that you are doing all you can to achieve efficiencies and focus your energy and that of your staff on service over process, the real task of the library leaders is to sustain support for the existing collections, while pushing forward new initiatives–no matter how small those new investments. There are many individuals (often hundreds of them in any one research library) focusing on the specifics, lobbying for their area. It is challenging, but you must synthesize these needs and desires and shift your attention to the larger picture. In a way, it is like assembling one of those pictures from a million different photos. You can end up with just a million different photos or with a bigger, grander picture that emerges from these many individual efforts. And there is so much more we could do if we look at this bigger picture: shared campus-wide investments in new technologies, and collections; investments in experiments and collaborations leading to entirely new forms of scholarly communication; shared help desk and IT support infrastructures. Every little step contributes to moving up the mountain! Do such strategies work? You bet they do: the University of Illinois at Urbana Champaign library was held harmless on the budget cuts and recessions. In the CIC, presses and libraries are working together to lead an effort to transform publishing on our campuses–with funding and support from the provosts.

When I look back over these past 10 years, we've made enormous strides as a profession in meeting the demands of the digital age–in spite of the dire predictions of many. Your message about scholarly communication has been heard and understood, new partnerships are emerging–with IT divisions, with presses, with colleges–to develop entirely new services. Share your love and passion for your work with everyone. It is absolutely infectious and an essential ingredient to your ultimate success.

Fishing the Electronic River: Disruptive Technologies, the Unlibrary, and the Ecology of Information

Dennis Dillon

SUMMARY. Provides the reader with ways in which to successfully locate, hook, and retrieve needed information in the electronic world. Discusses how libraries, the Internet, and e-books are all inter-related parts of the information ecology. *[Article copies available for a fee from The Haworth Document Delivery Service: 1-800-HAWORTH. E-mail address: <getinfo@haworth pressinc.com> Website: <http://www.HaworthPress.com> © 2002 by The Haworth Press, Inc. All rights reserved.]*

KEYWORDS. Electronic information, information ecology, technology

INTRODUCTION

Imagine you are on a voyage of discovery going up a river in a boat with four doctors, a fisherman, Groucho Marx's dog, a librarian, and Yogi Berra. The goal of your expedition is to seek out the headwaters of information, the original source not only of the electronic river, but the starting point of all knowledge.

The doctors stop and get out of the boat to go duck hunting. Together in the duck blind, they decide that instead of all shooting away at the same time, they would take turns as each duck came by. The first to have a shot would be the general practitioner, next would be the internist, then the surgeon, and finally the pathologist.

Dennis Dillon is Head, Collections and Information Resources, Perry-Castaneda Library, University of Texas at Austin, Austin, TX 78713-8916.

[Haworth co-indexing entry note]: "Fishing the Electronic River: Disruptive Technologies, the Unlibrary, and the Ecology of Information." Dillon, Dennis. Co-published simultaneously in *Journal of Library Administration* (The Haworth Information Press, an imprint of The Haworth Press, Inc.) Vol. 36, No. 3, 2002, pp. 45-58; and: *Electronic Resources and Collection Development* (ed: Sul H. Lee) The Haworth Information Press, an imprint of The Haworth Press, Inc., 2002, pp. 45-58. Single or multiple copies of this article are available for a fee from The Haworth Document Delivery Service [1-800-HAWORTH, 9:00 a.m. - 5:00 p.m. (EST). E-mail address: getinfo@haworthpressinc.com].

When the first bird flew over, the general practitioner lifted his shot-gun, but never fired, saying, "I'm not sure that was a duck."

The second bird was the internist's. He aimed and followed the bird in his sights, saying, "It looks like a duck, it flies like a duck, it sounds like a duck . . . ," but then the bird was out of range and the internist didn't take a shot.

As soon as the third bird appeared, flying up out of the water only a few feet from the blind, the surgeon blasted away, emptying his pump gun and blowing the bird to smithereens. Turning to the pathologist, the surgeon said, "Go see whether that was a duck."[1]

Different doctors, different interpretations of what they had seen and how to react. A librarian in the same situation would be very cautious about declaring just any flying object to be a duck, while to a Web search engine, everything in the sky would be classified as a duck.

Can we use this anecdote about personal information processing styles to generalize about human behavior, about how a researcher who is looking for information on ducks might begin a fruitful search?

Or to bring this question into better focus by quoting Groucho Marx's advice about information boundaries, "Outside of a dog, a book is a man's best fried. Inside of a dog it is too dark to read."[2] Groucho's remark points out as only he can, the importance of boundaries. Conditions are different outside of a dog than they are inside of a dog. It matters which side of a boundary you are on. And if you are doing duck research, it matters whether you begin in a database of biological research or a database of cooking recipes.

This paper however, is not about dogs or ducks, it is about rivers of electronic information.

RIVERS OF INFORMATION

From time immemorial rivers have been a metaphor for both conti-nuity and unceasing change. In Indian treaties the United States used the words:

> As long as the moon shall rise
>
> As long as the rivers shall flow[3]

Today we are going to take a trip up a river of electronic information. For any river traveler there are two rivers: the top inch of the river that you can see, and the larger, unknowable river that flows beneath the surface. One river is mapped, and the other is not. Just as with the ins and outs of Groucho's dog, it is possible to see and interpret what lies on the surface of the river, but it is not easy to divine what lies hidden underneath.

For those of us born into the print world, fishing for information in the electronic river of the Web is like casting a line into the darkness of another dimension. How can we hope to locate, hook, and retrieve the information we need? Sometimes we sit for long stretches, barely moving, staring at a computer screen, our eyes scanning the ripples of the electronic river, scrolling through screen after screen of text looking for a sign that will point us to the information we need. Of fishermen it is said, "there's a fine line between fishing and just standing on the shore like an idiot."[4] From the perspective of the fish, the difference between the motionless figure on shore with a fishing rod in hand, and the motionless figure on shore with a wireless laptop in hand, is slight. And neither figure is guaranteed to retrieve what they seek.

Fish lie on the other side of a border. It is more than just a simple border separating tweedledum from tweedledee, for the fish inhabit a different medium. A fisherman on the river can no more be certain of a fish's location than a searcher can know what lies across the Internet's border or what flows undetected underneath the Internet's surface. The fish of the electronic river are untamed, unmapped, and frequently lacking in manners or metadata. Unlike your spouse, a fish does not come when called, unlike your children it does not go to bed when told, and unlike captured data in your OPAC, it does not respond to your erstwhile attempts to retrieve it.

When questioned about his techniques for locating fish however, the gruff old fisherman on our boat will only allow that, "fishing with me, has always been an excuse to drink in the daytime."[5] But Groucho's dog knows better. A fisherman guesses. He casts to where his instincts and suspicions tell him the fish will be on that particular day. He calculates which species are likely to be in any particular stretch of water. In selecting his bait, he uses educated hunches long-honed from previous encounters. He hopes his strategies, skills, and knowledge will lead to success; that a fish will take the bait. That luck will be on his side as he sets the hook and starts the retrieval.

It is a process, considers the librarian, not unlike that used by my colleagues when they fish the electronic river, casting baited keywords into a database hoping to catch a bit of slippery information.

For the fisherman this is a contest that takes place in two simultaneous dimensions, in the water and out, the fisherman linked to the fish only through intuition and delicate signals in his line. The invisible fish in one dimension, the unseeing fisherman in another. For both the librarian and the fisherman, failure is a familiar companion. As Samuel Johnson said three hundred years ago, "A fishing rod is a stick with a hook on one end and a fool at the other."[6] This feeling of frustration is one that every librarian can identify with, since most of them have struggled trying to hook an elusive electronic record that they know is lurking beneath the surface, but that cannot be enticed out of the electronic river's depths with any bait at their command.

INFORMATION ECOLOGY I

The electronic river is part of the information ecosystem. In this ecosystem, readers read, publishers publish, authors write, librarians collect, and information technologists think that all of these things should be done with computers. There are different viewpoints among all of us in the information ecosystem, just as there are among the four doctors on our boat, yet we are friendly neighbors. However, G. K. Chesterton notes, "Your next-door neighbor is not a man; he is an environment. He is the barking of a dog, he is the noise of a piano; he is a dispute about a wall; he is drains that are worse than yours, or roses that are better than yours."[7] What your neighbor thinks and does matters. Within the information community, the activities of our neighbors have consequences. When publishers produce e-books and e-journals, libraries respond. When our colleagues on the Internet create a better search engine, libraries take note. The inter-relationships within this community form the information ecology. It is an ecology in which every member of the information community has their traditional niche. But nowadays libraries are also publishers, publishers are also booksellers, and so forth and so on. The comfortable boundaries and ecological niches that have traditionally distinguished all of us from one another, that have provided the justification for our existence, are shifting. It is within this context that some of the questions of this paper arise.

1. Where does the library begin?
2. What is the opposite of library?
3. What is the source of the electronic river?
4. What if Groucho's dog eats the last existing copy of an e-book?

BORDERS

"So," wonders the librarian, "where do the borders of the library begin? Do they begin at the library's front door, at the library Web page, at the library card in a patron's wallet, at the MARC record tagged with the library OCLC symbol? Does the library begin where the Internet ends, or does it begin with a child's first check-out? Is the library wherever the librarian happens to be? Is the library a collection, or a service, or an information organization?"

Peter Drucker, looking ahead to the near future and writing in the *Economist* a few months ago, talked about boundaries and noted that "every institution in the knowledge society–not only businesses, but also schools, universities, hospitals and increasingly government agencies too–has to be globally competitive, even though most organizations will continue to be local in their activities and in their markets. This is because the Internet will keep customers everywhere informed on what is available anywhere in the world."[8]

Does this mean that to be effective, every library has to be globally competitive? To take this view is a different way of approaching our traditional responsibilities, though we have always made use of union catalogs, reached out to worldwide resources through interlibrary loan, and referred users to other institutions and sources of information. To some extent, every library has always been a local branch of the worldwide library, so perhaps new conditions do not require much of a change after all. Perhaps the library's boundaries are not geographical, but ideological?

Libraries began in an age when information was scarce. Do we need to adjust our mission now that information is so plentiful that it is frequently a nuisance, when the wealthy flee to remote corners of the globe in order to escape from information, to escape from a world filled with telephones, television, newspapers, and endless e-mail chatter?

Last year at the Frankfurt Book Fair, Tom Peters noted that libraries are experiencing a large, long-term revolution. He said, "In one sense they are still medieval, viewing information as scarce, precious and stable, focusing on the value of collections. Now of course, there is a glut of information that is not static, and does not need to reside in any one particular space."[9]

The usual public relations response to questions about library borders and library change is to say that the mission of libraries is to serve the information needs of their user populations, and that over time, libraries will adapt their efforts to meet the changing needs of this population.

Most of us would probably say that the reality is that we are no longer sure what the borders of the library should be. In the book, *Childhood's Future*, Richard Louy has noted that, "Not too many years ago, a child's experience was limited by how far he or she could ride a bicycle or by the physical boundaries that parents set. Today . . . the real boundaries of a child's life are set more by the number of available cable channels, by the simulated reality of video games, by the number of megabytes of memory in the home computer. Now kids can go anywhere, as long as they stay inside the electronic bubble."[10]

As the boundaries between those of us in the information business keep crumbling however, it is useful to remember an additional warning from G. K. Chesterton, who said, "Don't take down a fence unless you know why it was put up in the first place."[11] Today we not only face questions about the reasons for pre-existing information boundaries, we are also called upon to establish boundaries in areas we've never operated in before.

How far should we stray from home? Should a library be a publisher? Should an electronic publisher be an archive? Dogs that stray too far from home get lost. Organizations without boundaries and limits fall victim to never ending demands and mission creep, ending up trying to be all things to all people and losing their focus. Yet all of us in the information ecology can feel the winds of change on the backs of our necks and have concerns about what our borders should be.

DISRUPTIVE TECHNOLOGIES

Businesses today are very aware of changes occurring in their ecosystems and on their borders.

When the telephone was first introduced, President Rutherford Hayes said, "That's an amazing invention, but who would ever want to use one of them?"[12] Western Union, the telegraph company, ignored the telephone since it could only carry a signal three miles, and their telegraph operators considered it a toy with no future. Yet within five years, *Scientific American* was saying that the telephone would bring a greater "kinship of humanity" and cause "nothing less than a new organization of society." By that time others were worrying that telephones would "spread germs through the wires, destroy local accents, and give authoritarian governments a listening box in the homes of their subjects."[13]

The telephone is an example of what is known as a disruptive technology. Disruptive technologies are innovations that suddenly alter expectations and behavior to such a degree that the existing competing institutions within its ecosystem are simply incapable of adapting. Western Union, like so many companies since, faltered when faced with a disruptive technology, not because they were ineptly managed, but precisely because they were well managed. They made two mistakes, they listened to their customers who wanted more and better telegraph connections, and they focused their company energy on the most profitable and highly used part of their business instead of paying attention to developments on their borders. Western Union had a vast, successful international infrastructure devoted to the telegraph, and virtually none of their customers had the slightest interest in the telephone. Like all classic disruptive technologies, the telephone allowed less skilled people to do things that previously required the assistance of expensive specialists in centralized and inconvenient locations.[14]

Parallels to our own field of expertise leap immediately to mind. Do authors really want to put their fate into the hands of remote multi-national publishers? Do information seekers really want to drive to the library or try to decipher our hundreds of databases? Do scholars really want to send their articles to painfully slow, distant, journals with exclusive and expensive distribution systems?

INFORMATION ECOLOGY II

Just as the effects of disruptive technologies can be devastating to existing industries, the introduction of disruptive species within an ecosystem can be equally dangerous. Take for example, the well-known stories about the horrors that have resulted when baby alligators have been mistakenly introduced into the sewers beneath our great cities. Unchecked by the normal forces of sewer ecology, these mythic alligators have grown to enormous size feeding on small pets, errant children, and unaware and disbelieving adults. Just as disruptive technologies make it difficult for industry competitors to adjust, disruptive species make it difficult for competing species in the ecosystem to adjust.

Other classic examples of ecological disruption that can stand up to a higher degree of scrutiny include the introduction of rabbits into Australia, Kudzu into the American south, and Zebra Mussels into the ecology of the Great Lakes. In each of these cases, the new disruptive species changed the local ecology, displacing the pre-existing species that used to inhabit the same ecological niche, just as the telephone displaced the telegraph, the alphabet displaced hieroglyphics, and the printing press displaced the hand copying of manuscripts.

THE NATURE OF DISCOVERY

As we rejoin our friends on the river we discover that they no longer know where they are. Yogi is steering. The general practitioner says, "Yogi, I think we're lost." Yogi replies, "Yeah, but we're making great time."[15]

The doctors, looking for help from the crew, find the librarian and the fisherman engaged in conversation. "Take the tarpon, for instance," says the fisherman. "They begin appearing off Key West in early spring. No one is sure where they came from. They can be larger than a football player, yet are usually taken in less than three feet of water by fly fishermen on a half-ounce lure. A stranded Tarpon can breathe air for days until it finds its way back to deep water. Tarpon are of this earth, but they are unpredictable, inscrutable, and in every sense of the word, wild."

"Just like books," says the librarian, "they can spring up from anywhere at anytime. They are often attributed to authors who don't really exist, and published by companies that have vanished from the face of the earth. Librarians try to corral the wild ones by securing them in our databases, but the nimble ones escape and remain forever at large. New books can erupt like a force of nature at anytime and anyplace–and like the Tarpon, they must be pursued when glimpsed, for we may never see them again."

Groucho's dog got up and walked to the bow of the boat where it was quiet, he thought, "Librarians and fishermen don't have the sense of a dog." He kept his eyes peeled on the narrowing of the river channel and the increase in the river current as the cliffs began to close in around them. The humans droned on in the background. Groucho's dog mused, "Even a dog knows that when you are on a boat in an electronic river, you better pay attention to what is happening around you." As the wind picked up, a wave of icy water drenched the fisherman and librarian who had been lost in a discussion about the details of digitizing a series of fishing books.

The belatedly aware librarian noticed that the electronic river was rapidly filling with e-books bobbing in the water as far as the eye could see, dark and foreboding, colliding against the hull with dull thunks like the knock of the grim reaper on his victim's door.

The books had escaped their boundaries. Previously confined to print, they were now free to reproduce and proliferate in the electronic river. A twenty-volume encyclopedia struck the port bow spilling the doctors off their seats. Groucho's dog, alarmed by the fragile boat's nearness to eternity, began barking furiously.

Concerns that had previously seemed so important vanished from everyone's minds. Afloat on the electronic river, assailed by uncontrollable changes in the weather, assaulted by undomesticated e-books, they had no defense against the allied forces beyond their control except their own limited knowledge, blind luck, and sheer doggedness.

The fisherman said, "The Quakers have a maxim to guide them through life's obstacles, they say, 'Proceed as the way opens.' "[16] Yogi, steering deftly and guided by the fisherman's words, dodged the threats around them and held a steady course up river towards the headwaters of all knowledge.

E-BOOKS

So what about e-books? Are e-books a noxious information weed that will destroy pre-existing information forms and wreck havoc upon a delicately balanced information ecology that has worked well for generations?

Longtime New York publishing icon, Jason Epstein, has noted that publishing today is controlled by a handful of large multi-national corporations that are a result of the peculiar business conditions of print-based publishing, and which inspire little author or reader loyalty. The current system, Epstein says, is an "over concentrated and inefficient literary marketplace dominated by book chains and rooted in the five-hundred-year-old Gutenberg system of centralized manufacture and physical distribution."[17]

With traditional author royalties running between twenty to thirty percent of a publisher's net revenues, and another forty percent or so of revenues absorbed by executive, administrative, and overhead costs, traditional publishers are bloated with the inefficiencies necessary for the sustenance of print. Their ability to maneuver is limited by the high profits expected by corporate ownership. They have little freedom to move into areas that won't return quick profits, and little time to devote to new authors, non-traditional customers, or to explore new ways of doing business. They are dependent on the existing economics of print publishing in order to supply the revenues needed to continue their current operations.

In the new emerging e-book publishing model, however, an author can supply digital files to a publisher who then adds only minimal editorial and design value to the manuscript, converts it to a secure e-book format, and then sells the e-book or print-on-demand title directly to the customer. In comparison to traditional publishing, this new approach allows author royalties to be increased, the retail price of the book to the consumer to be decreased, and the publisher's administrative and overhead costs to be reduced. Everybody wins.

Because these new companies are unburdened with the overhead necessary to sustain print publishing, they can outbid traditional publishers for authors by offering author royalties of seventy percent or more, while simultaneously lowering retail prices to the customer. Using print-on-demand technology they can sell a printed bound book to customers at a cost of less than five dollars, or provide that same customer with the option of receiving the book in a variety of different e-book formats.

Because of the proliferation of e-book middlemen that can handle online sales, digital conversion, and produce printed books on demand, the new e-book publishers can outsource all of these functions and keep their overhead costs to a minimum. Since they are doing business in a different way, these new publishers are able to take chances on unknown authors, and devote more time and energy to their customers.

By employing a model that subverts traditional publishing and that provides substantial advantages for both the author and reader, the new publishers have mixed disruptive technologies in original ways and have come up with an approach to publishing that is part vanity press, part independent bookstore, and part neighborhood publisher. And once these books are in the databases of online retailers like Amazon.com, these small publishers benefit from the same global market reach as the large traditional publishers.

While the sales of these new e-book presses are relatively small, e-book events are following the classic script blazed by other disruptive technologies. Traditional publishers are acutely aware of the dangers on their borders, but they are held captive by the demands of their existing business model. In some respects they are in the position of the turtle that was mugged and robbed by a gang of snails. When the police asked the turtle for a description of the villains, the turtle replied, "I'm sorry, I just don't know. It all happened so fast." The publishers are moving slowly because the existing print model still works fine, just like the telegraph worked just fine when the telephone was first invented.

But publishers can see that things are likely to change. They do have one potential ace in the hole that may allow them to transition to the e-book gracefully over time, and that is the library market. The library market potentially provides them with an arena in which to experiment with e-books, develop a predictable revenue stream, and painlessly create a mainstream consumer base that is comfortable with e-books because they have used them in their libraries.

A RECONSIDERATION

Lets reconsider the main elements of our story so far.

a. Libraries, the Internet, and e-books are all inter-related parts of the information ecology.
b. Disruptive technologies can change this ecology. Publisher's come, publishers go. Formats come, formats go. Every species within the information ecosystem has to constantly adjust to the activities of its neighbors.
c. Borders are important, but borders change. Ecological niches change. The disruptive technologies brought about by the Internet and print-on-demand technology, are likely to have a profound effect upon publishing. Anything that affects publishing will have a profound affect upon libraries.
d. Within the information ecosystem not every species has been tamed and corralled. In library terms, few of our neighbors in the information ecosystem have metadata. But as Yogi says, "If the world were perfect, it wouldn't be."[18] Everything will never be in a single database. And libraries, which by their very nature must have borders, can not contain everything.
e. And, of course, as Yogi would say, "You got to be careful if you don't know where you're going, because you might not get there."[19]

ON THE BOAT

But back to our friends on the boat as they near the source waters from which all information springs. Remember the duck hunting doctors? Let's begin with the pathologist's report on what the surgeon really did shoot out of the sky.

" So Doc," asked the librarian, "was it a duck?"

"Well, no," replied the pathologist, "I'm afraid it was tarpon. It was leaping out of the water with the fisherman's hook still in his mouth, and the surgeon shot it."

"Its not always easy to tell a duck from a fish," said the librarian, "which reminds me of a story."

"You talk too much," said the fisherman.

"But this has to do with our journey to find the source of all knowledge," said the librarian. "It is a story about true knowledge and false knowledge, and about knowing whether you are shooting a duck or a tarpon."

"I'm interested," said the pathologist.

"Well," said the librarian, "when *London Times* reporters walked through an abandoned Al Qaeda safe house in Kabul during November 2001, they found documents indicating that the Al Qaeda had been trying to build a nuclear bomb. When the reporters held up one of the articles to the BBC cameras covering their examination, audience members immediately identified the article as one published in the Science satire magazine, the *Journal of Irreproducible Results*. Because they weren't native English speakers, the Al Qaeda didn't realize that the entire A-bomb article was a joke."[20]

"So after doing their research, they weren't able to distinguish fact from fiction," said the pathologist.

"Exactly," said the librarian, "when someone searches the entire information ecosystem, they are as likely to retrieve fiction as fact, as likely to shoot a tarpon as a duck. The key is having the background and judgement to know the difference."

The river was becoming too shallow for the boat. Our travelers got out and walked through the grass until they came to the spring that was the headwaters of the electronic river. A stone monument rose nearby. Upon it were engraved the words, "In the beginning was the word, and all information flows from it."

"Wen Ming," said the librarian.

"What?" asked the fisherman.

"Wen Ming," said the librarian, "it is the word for civilization in Chinese. It means literally, *understanding writing*."[21]

"In other words," said the pathologist, "the source of the electronic river is civilization. In the beginning was the Word,[22] so to speak."

"Well, that's one mystery solved," said the fisherman.

"Weren't we also looking for the opposite of library?" asked the surgeon.

"Yes, but that's easy," said the librarian, "a library is a focused and organized subset of human information, the opposite of library is the unfocused, unorganized, totality of human information–or in other words, the entire information ecosystem."

"So where does the library begin?" asked the general practitioner.

"That's a snap," said the librarian, "the library begins wherever the librarian wants it to. For better or worse, the librarian sets the boundaries of the library."

"Our journey is over and it looks like we've answered all our questions. Let's go home," said the pathologist.

"Wait a minute," said the surgeon, "I think the dog just ate the last electronic copy of the *Physician's Desk Reference*."

"So shoot him," said the fisherman, "you already shot my tarpon. No book last forever. Nothing lasts forever. Loss and decay is just nature's way of taking out the trash. If we didn't lose things or throw them away, we wouldn't even be able to walk for all the stuff piled up around us."

"Dead men walking," added the pathologist, "can disrupt the living."

And so as our tale comes to a close, the four doctors, the librarian, the fisherman, and Groucho's dog, all turned to the Captain, Yogi Berra, whose unerring instincts had brought their journey to a successful conclusion.

They asked, "Do you have any last words Yogi?"

"Of course," said Yogi, "Just remember this the next time you are on the electronic river, in theory there is no difference between theory and practice. In practice there is."[23]

NOTES

1. Cohen, Ted. *Jokes: philosophical thoughts on joking matters*, (Chicago: The University of Chicago Press, 1999). 13.

2. Groucho Marx quoted in the Quotations Page (http://www.quotationspage.com/).

3. Anonymous, quoted in John Bartlett. *Familiar quotations: a collection of passages, phrases, and proverbs traced to their sources in ancient and modern literature*, (Boston: Little, Brown, 1992) p 787.

4. Stephen Wright quoted in the Quotations Page (http://www.quotationspage.com/).

5. Jimmy Cannon quoted in the Quotations Page (http://www.quotationspage.com/).

6. Samuel Johnson quoted in the Quotations Page (http://www.quotationspage.com/).

7. Chesterton, G. K quoted in *Columbia World of Quotations* (New York: Columbia University Press, 1996).

8. Drucker, Peter. "The Next Society," *The Economist*, November 1st 2001.

9. Lichtenberg, James. "Libraries Look for Niche in Electronic-Publishing World," *Publisher's Weekly* 9/24/2001.

10. Louv, Richard. *Childhood's Future*, (Boston: Houghton Mifflin, 1990.) part 8, ch. 4.

11. G. K. Chesterton quoted in John Bartlett. *Familiar quotations: a collection of passages, phrases, and proverbs traced to their sources in ancient and modern literature*, (Boston: Little, Brown, 1968) p 918.

12. *The Experts speak: the definitive compendium of authoritative misinformation* (New York: Pantheon Books, 1984) 206.

13. Rosenzweig, Roy. "Live Free or Die? Death Life, Survival, and Sobriety on the Information Superhighway." *American Quarterly* 51.1 (1999) 160-174.

14. "Disruption is Good (Interview with Clayton Christensen)," *CIO Magazine*, April 1, 2001. http://www.cio.com/archive/040101/disruption_content.html.

15. Yogi Berra quotes were from the following Web sites: (http://www.yogi-berra.com/yogiisms.html) (http://www.yogiberraclassic.org/quotes.htm) (http://www.workinghumor.com/quotes/yogi_berra.shtml).

16. Heat Moon, William Least. *River-horse: the logbook of a boat across America*, (Boston: Houghton Mifflin,1999)–Proceed as way opens–need to find page.

17. Epstein, Jason. In "Reading: The Digital Future," http://www.text-e.org/.

18. Yogi Berra quotes were from the following Web sites: (http://www.yogi-berra.com/yogiisms.html) (http://www.yogiberraclassic.org/quotes.htm) (http://www.workinghumor.com/quotes/yogi_berra.shtml).

19. Yogi Berra quotes were from the following Web sites: (http://www.yogi-berra.com/yogiisms.html) (http://www.yogiberraclassic.org/quotes.htm) (http://www.workinghumor.com/quotes/yogi_berra.shtml).

20. "Taliban Thwarted by Irreproducible Result." *The Daily Rotten*, November 16, 2001. http://www.dailyrotten.com/archive/159929.html.

21. Snyder, Gary. *Gary Snyder Reader; prose, poetry, and translations, 1952-1998*, (Washington, DC: Counterpoint, 1999) 315.

22. *The Bible*. The Gospel According to John. 1:1.

23. Yogi Berra quotes were from the following Web sites: (http://www.yogi-berra.com/yogiisms.html) (http://www.yogiberraclassic.org/quotes.htm) (http://www.workinghumor.com/quotes/yogi_berra.shtml).

Collection Development
for Distance Learning

Anne Marie Casey

SUMMARY. Discusses collection development for distance learning in both the print and electronic era. Focuses on several advances in electronic access that have impacted collection development in recent years. *[Article copies available for a fee from The Haworth Document Delivery Service: 1-800-HAWORTH. E-mail address: <getinfo@haworthpressinc.com> Website: <http://www.HaworthPress.com> © 2002 by The Haworth Press, Inc. All rights reserved.]*

KEYWORDS. Collection development, distance learning, CD-ROMs, World Wide Web

The *ACRL Guidelines for Distance Learning Library Services* (ACRL 2000) defines distance learning library services as, " . . . those . . . in support of college, university, or other post-secondary courses and programs offered away from a main campus, or in the absence of a traditional campus, and regardless of where credit is given. These courses may be taught in traditional or non-traditional formats or media, may or may not require physical facilities, and may or may not involve live interaction of teachers and students. The phrase is inclusive of courses in all post-secondary programs designated as extension, extended, off-campus, extended campus, distance, distributed, open, flexible, franchising, virtual, synchronous, or asynchronous."

Anne Marie Casey is Director, Off-Campus Library Services, Central Michigan University, Mount Pleasant, MI 48859.

[Haworth co-indexing entry note]: "Collection Development for Distance Learning." Casey, Anne Marie. Co-published simultaneously in *Journal of Library Administration* (The Haworth Information Press, an imprint of The Haworth Press, Inc.) Vol. 36, No. 3, 2002, pp. 59-72; and: *Electronic Resources and Collection Development* (ed: Sul H. Lee) The Haworth Information Press, an imprint of The Haworth Press, Inc., 2002, pp. 59-72. Single or multiple copies of this article are available for a fee from The Haworth Document Delivery Service [1-800-HAWORTH, 9:00 a.m. - 5:00 p.m. (EST). E-mail address: getinfo@haworthpressinc.com].

This is a very broad definition and necessarily so because distance learning programs in higher education are provided in a multitude of ways. Some of these lend themselves to the provision of library services much more easily than others. For example, at a branch campus where a physical library exists, it is far simpler to extend basic library services to students who live in close proximity to that branch than it is to a sole student taking a correspondence course in a remote area. One of the great challenges in defining ideal library services to the remote learner has been that conditions vary greatly in the type of programs libraries must serve and in the funding available to do so.

In the last decade, with the advances in technology and the widespread accessibility to it, distance learning library services have become more standardized and grown closer to traditional library services as they too offer more materials electronically. The most efficient way to provide information to remote students today is through the World Wide Web. This is as true for on-campus "distance" students and faculty researching from dorm rooms, offices, and homes as it is for the true distance learner who is at a significant geographic distance from the campus library. There are some differences in the collection development patterns for electronic resources for distance learners but these are not as significant as the patterns were before their proliferation.

To understand the collection development of electronic resources in today's libraries that serve distance students, it would be helpful to see them in the context of collection development for distance learning programs in print-based libraries.

COLLECTION DEVELOPMENT FOR DISTANCE LEARNING IN THE "PRINT ERA"

In a review of the literature, the amount of material written on collection development for distance learning library services is small and consists to a large degree of case studies. The small body of literature concerned with collection development and distance learning is logical in light of the fact that the most prominent concerns of distance learning librarians have been the dissemination of information to remote students and faculty rather than the collection of it. The literature traditionally has focused on instruction, reference, and document delivery. Especially in academic institutions where distance learning courses are the same as those taught on-campus, although often in different formats, the prime objective has been to get the material that already existed in the library collection out to the distant students.

Traditionally, distance learning library services have not had the resources to focus on much other than the immediate needs of filling remote students' requests as quickly as possible. It is often the case that staffing devoted to distance learning students in libraries is minimal. Many libraries have small numbers of staff devoted to distance learners or staff who split their responsibilities between on-campus and distance learning needs. Distance learning librarians have historically left collection development to their on-campus colleagues because they needed to focus their limited resources on the delivery of library materials. At Central Michigan University (CMU), Off-Campus Library Services (OCLS) is a separate department that provides library services and materials exclusively to students and faculty in off-campus or distance learning programs. OCLS librarians have relied on the libraries' subject bibliographers to maintain the collections and have added to them primarily in the areas only taught off-campus, such as vehicle design administration.

In spite of the small body of literature on collection development for distance learning library services, those that are available give a good picture of the collection development practices in the print era. Despite differences in approaches, some trends evolve in the ways that libraries all over the world handled collections for distance learners. The library services described in these articles vary in some ways, but appear to have had a common approach to collection development in the pre-electronic days. This approach can be summed up in three phrases–multiple copies, deposit collections, and referrals. The most consistent trends in early distance learning library services were to collect multiple copies of books that were requested by distance learning students, to deposit core collections of materials in places that were close to clusters of distance students, and to refer students to other libraries in their areas.

Collecting multiple copies of books that appeared on the reading lists of faculty in the distance programs was often determined to be the best way to deal with the competing needs of students on-campus with easy access to the library and students off-campus who needed longer borrowing times to compensate for mailing. Some libraries, such as Deakin University and the University of New England in Australia as well as the University of South Africa, devised formulae for the number of copies that the library should purchase based on the number of students registered in distance learning courses (McKnight 1998; Schmude and Luxton 1986; Willemse 1986). From 1955-1970, when the University of New England Collection for distance students was housed at the State Library in Sydney, it was not unheard of for up to 50 copies of the same book to be purchased (Schmude and Luxton 1986). At the University of Manitoba, to support courses taken off-campus, copies were added quickly to the library's collection by purchasing the books at the university bookstore so they would be on the shelves as fast as possible (Angel and Budnick 1986). National University in California, where the author was employed from 1987-1991 and functioned as head of serials, purchased multiple subscriptions to periodicals to be placed at each of the branch campus libraries. The University of British Columbia maintained a separate, uncatalogued Extension Collection, which consisted of duplicates of books in the library's collection (Whitehead 1987). At CMU, OCLS maintains a small uncatalogued collection of multiple copies of titles that are frequently requested and, in the past, also maintained a separate collection of textbooks for faculty to review while preparing for courses (Garrett 1988).

The establishment of smaller library collections in areas where distance learning classes were offered has been another common way to ensure that students would have ready access to the most important materials needed for their studies. There are numerous avenues for establishing local site collections. Park University in Missouri established local collections of books, periodicals, and audio-visual materials at the base libraries of the military installations on which its courses were taught (Peterman and Schultis 1993). Old Dominion University in Virginia set up core collections in the community college libraries where it had partnerships (Pettingill 1998). Laurentian University in Ontario moved core collections around by sending them to the areas in which a course was being taught and moving them when the course was over. It also established some permanent core collections in local libraries that were given honoraria for their assistance (Kelly 1987). The Open University of Sri Lanka and Sukhothai Thammathirat Open University in Thailand both set up small core collections in designated public libraries throughout their countries (Wijesinghe 1988; Cusripituck and Puttapithakporn 1988). Small remote center libraries were established at Deakin University, the University of the South Pacific, the University of Queensland in Australia, and Indira Ghandi National Open University in India (Day and Angus 1986; Campbell 1988; Williams 1986; Kanjilal and Tripathi 1995). The University of Wyoming set up a major branch library in Casper and also purchased materials to be housed in a community college library where one distance learning program was offered (Johnson 1987). CMU donated subscriptions to appropriate indexes to military libraries and other local libraries in areas where classes were held.

The third approach to collections that distance learning libraries have taken was referral to other libraries. This could be done in a variety of ways. In the days of primarily print-based libraries, it was common practice to informally refer students to libraries in their home areas that might have collections that would be useful to them. Until the late 1990s, CMU librarians visited the major libraries in each of the areas where classes were taught whenever they traveled to those areas for instruction. Normally the visits took place annually. They maintained library guides that described the collections available at all of the local libraries and handed them out to students at instruction classes. Although many distance learning library services have ceased to informally refer students to other libraries, it is not uncommon today to click on a distance learning library services link on a major academic library's Web page and find a list of libraries open to the public in the areas where that institution offers courses. The *Guidelines for Distance Learning Library Services* (ACRL 2000) states that it is the responsibility of the sponsoring institution to provide library services and materials to its students, so most libraries provide informal referrals only as an adjunct to their main services.

Many distance learning library services also contract with other organizations to provide materials to their students. Of the 169 respondents to the questionnaire for the *Off-Campus Library Services Directory*, 3rd ed., 73 referred their students to commercial document providers and 85 arranged library privileges at local libraries for distance learning students at their institutions (Casey and Cachero 1998). Contracting with other organizations may become more of a trend in the future as companies such as Jones e-Global Library are created to provide library services, for a fee, to institutions that are not able to set up appropriate distance learning library services of their own (Heilig 2001).

COLLECTION DEVELOPMENT FOR DISTANCE LEARNING IN THE "ELECTRONIC ERA"

Some of the earliest electronic materials to appear in distance learning library services were subscriptions to electronic databases for the librarians who provided support. Library services subscribed to collections of online databases, such as DIALOG and BRS, so that the librarians could perform mediated database searches for the students. In the 1980s, libraries began to subscribe to individual indexes on CD-ROMs. The yearly subscription rates for the indexes on CD-ROM were generally more cost-effective than the online connect charges for database collections.

In 1987, Cardinal Stritch College in Wisconsin subscribed to Infotrac and Business Collection, a set of full text articles, on CD-ROM. The librarians began sending mediated searches to distance students from these databases rather than from the more costly DIALOG. In 1988, students surveyed were very satisfied with the search results. The librarians were able to do more extensive searching on the CD-ROMs because they did not have to worry about online charges. They also were able to fill a substantial number of requests for articles from the Business Collection rather than turning to ILL to fill them (Ruddy 1988).

At CMU, the OCLS librarians in each of the regional library offices had subscriptions to at least two bibliographic databases on CD-ROM and added new subscriptions as needed to cover new disciplines or geographic areas. They used the CD-ROM databases for mediated searches and only turned to the online services for the odd topic that was not found on the CD-ROMs. As in the case of Cardinal Stritch College, the OCLS librarians were able to do far more extensive searches when they did not have to worry about connect charges.

As well as providing mediated searches for distance learning students, some library services also placed CD-ROMs at remote sites. Park University purchased CD-ROMs to place in base libraries on installations where its courses were being taught. In FY 1992-1993, 36% of the Park University distance learning acquisitions budget was dedicated to this (Peterman and Schultis 1993). In a survey conducted in 1989 of distance learning librarians who had CD-ROMs in their libraries, 36% reported that they used the CD-ROMs for distance learning students. Of these, 73% used them from the main campus library while 27% had placed them at remote sites (Power 1992).

As more and more print materials, especially reference materials and indexes and abstracts, began to become available electronically, librarios devoted collection development money to them. Students in libraries found that the electronic indexes were easier to use than their print-based counterparts. Certainly a more complicated and sophisticated level of searching is possible in most electronic databases. Since distance learning students did not have easy access to library materials, the idea of making the electronic materials available to remote students was seemingly the answer to the perennial dilemma of providing students with timely and appropriate library materials.

In a paper presented at the 1998 International Conference on New Missions of Academic Libraries in the 21st Century, Uma Kanjilal sums up neatly the appeal of electronic or virtual libraries for the distance learner when she wrote, "The advantages of digital libraries from the point of view of distance learners are manifold. The basic advantages that one can see of such systems are that:

- They provide access to knowledge bases in a wide variety of media.
- They are accessible from the students' workplaces or homes, at their own convenient time, therefore cutting down the trip to different libraries.
- They help in avoiding the unnecessary duplication of material in different regional or study centers and making it a cost-effective mean (sic) of providing library services.
- They provide broader, faster and better delivery of sources and information.
- They can avoid loss of material in transit" (Kanjilal 1998, 3).

In order to make their electronic databases available to remote students, some libraries purchased systems that would make bibliographic databases available through their online public access catalogues (OPAC), which could be accessed remotely through a dial-up connection. In the mid 1990s, CMU launched its Infoshare system, which was part of the NOTIS OPAC. In addition to the libraries' catalogue, access to four databases, ERIC, IAC Expanded Academic Index, IAC Business Index, and PsychLIT, was made available via Infoshare. Remote students within the state of Michigan could dial into a statewide network for free to access the OPAC and databases. OCLS also paid for a free local access number that dialed into the Michigan system in the greater Washington, DC area, which had a significant concentration of CMU's distance learning student population in the early 1990s. Although access was available long-distance to CMU distance learning students in may other areas, it was not well used outside of Michigan and Washington, DC because of the cost and some complications with the dial-up process.

Difficulty in connecting to the libraries' online resources was a frustration a decade ago that slowed down accessibility on the part of distance learning students and active collection building of electronic resources on the part of distance learning librarians. In 1993, the University of St. Thomas in St. Paul, Minnesota embarked on a project to establish access for its distance learning students to the library's electronic system (Zietlow and Kragness 1993). One of the major obstacles to students' ability to set up an account to access the online library resources was that each student needed to apply at the Computing Center on campus during normal business hours. The extension librarian arranged for the distance learning students to apply through the remote site libraries and the librarians took on the responsibility of verifying that the students were eligible for accounts, a function normally done by the Computing Center. Despite the efforts of the librarians, only a small number of distance learning students had set up accounts at the time of the report. Those who did have accounts were still responsible for any long distance charges they incurred dialing into the system.

In the mid 1990s, the Internet emerged as the means to provide electronic resources to remote students in an easy way. Bibliographic databases, reference tools, periodicals and books became available on the World Wide Web. In some cases, the information on the World Wide Web was available free of charge to anyone. Most libraries started to construct Web pages that linked to freely available reference tools, books, journals, and other Web sites for their students. Subscription databases were also available and could generally be viewed by any student at a workstation in the library.

However, library site licenses for subscription materials generally restrict their use to members of an institution's community, such as students, faculty and staff. In general, the vendors set up access to any users on computers with an IP address registered with the vendor as valid for that institution. The IP addresses used are normally those of the computers in the library. Most libraries have set up systems to authenticate their remote users to enable them to access restricted databases. A common way to do this at the turn of the century has been to set up a proxy server that authenticates valid users and "fools" the vendor's computer into thinking that the user is at a computer with an IP address in the valid range. The ability to provide access to a substantial body of library material through the World Wide Web has revolutionized the collection development practices of distance learning library services.

In 1995, the CMU Libraries formed a cross departmental committee, the Automated Information Sources Access Committee (AISAC), to recommend a vendor for subscription databases that would be made available through the Libraries' Web site, which was under construction at the time. AISAC members solicited suggestions from library staff and faculty and arranged for vendors to demonstrate products at public meetings in the library. Select members of AISAC were charged with gathering additional information on particular vendors. After all of the information had been presented, AISAC was charged with delivering a recommendation of the best subscription service for CMU to the Dean of Libraries. This was a significant recommendation because of the amount of acquisitions dollars that would be pledged to one electronic system. At the final AISAC meeting where the decision was made about which vendor to recommend, the majority of committee members argued in favor of one product that had a sophisticated search engine and offered the subject matter in its databases that was the most important to CMU. However, the OCLS committee member argued in favor of recommending OCLC's new FirstSearch product, which at the time was the only one that was set up for easy accessibility by remote users. She pleaded her case to the committee that access outside the library was far more important to the distance learning population than to anyone else at the time, and it would be unwise to choose a vendor which would not be able to accommodate distance learning students. The committee agreed to recommend FirstSearch and the Dean followed through on this recommendation.

This illustrates an important change in the collection development practices in academic libraries in the last decade. Because of the enormous cost of major online resource subscriptions, the decisions in many libraries to acquire them have been made by cross-departmental committees. The needs of the distance learning users have been considered in a much more prominent way than they had in the past. Indeed, Ann Pettingill (1998) describes the process of selection decision-making at Old Dominion University by the electronic resources committee there as one in which the needs of the distance education population drove the process.

CMU regularly adds subscriptions to electronic resources to its collections. As the Head of Collection Development receives licenses for these to review, she examines them to be sure that they allow access to remote users. If they do not, CMU asks for a new license that does and will not subscribe to publications that will not change a license to allow access for remote users.

Another significant change brought on by the World Wide Web and the ability to set up remote authentication systems that can validate different groups of users into different subscription databases is that distance learning library services can now subscribe to resources that only the distance learning populations need and can set up their systems to validate only those users. This has enabled distance learning library services to have more independence in collection building.

Another area in which distance learning library services have used electronic methods to build their collections has been through the method of tracking requests. It has long been common in distance learning library services to perform mediated searches and send library materials directly to the students. Requests for reference support and document delivery traditionally have been captured in databases so that a very clear picture of the students' needs has emerged.

At CMU, the OCLS librarians historically practiced traditional collection development methods by reading reviews of new publications, participating in narrowly defined approval plans, and accepting requests from faculty members to a small degree. They also compiled bibliographies of books in the CMU collections that corresponded to classes being taught off-campus and so were able to recognize gaps in the book collections in particular areas and select new materials in those areas. However, a substantial amount of the OCLS acquisitions budget has traditionally been spent to maintain subscriptions to periodicals heavily used by distance learning students. Since all of the document delivery requests are captured in a database, yearly lists of requests of items not owned and requests that are filled are generated. Every year at subscription renewal time, the Director of OCLS, who is the libraries' subject bibliographer for distance learning collections, makes decisions about dropping expensive titles that are no longer requested heavily and about adding new titles that have had significant requests over a period of three to five years. The OCLS librarians also track reference requests and as patterns emerge for assignments that require particular sources of information, they attempt to locate electronic resources that will answer the students' needs. CMU is not unique in this approach to collection development. When San Jose State University in California established its Monterey County Campus, it set up a branch library with some collections that duplicated those at the main library. In the first year of operation, the staff studied student requests and ILL patterns to determine gaps in the branch campus library collection. They used this data to assist them in building the branch collection (Silveria and Leonard 1996).

This means of determining new materials to select is being advocated in libraries in general (Murphy and Rupp-Serrano 1999). Newer interlibrary loan software makes it easier to collect and analyze requests for items not owned in the library so that heavily requested items can be added to the collections. One author describes collection development based on patron demand as the "just in time solution" (Holleman 1998). In this case, traditional library services are beginning to adopt some of the collection development practices of their distance learning counterparts.

Another advance in electronic access that has impacted the collection development practices of the OCLS librarians is an increased dependence on ILL to supply materials not owned in the CMU collections. Over 90% of ILL article requests are received in two weeks or less because so many are now sent electronically. Since the off-campus courses at CMU are taught in compressed formats varying from five to eight weeks in length, traditional ILL turnaround times were not quick enough for OCLS to turn to ILL very often to supplement materials not held at the CMU Libraries. Beginning in November 1999, if a student has a minimum time of two weeks to wait for a document to be supplied and the material is not held at CMU, OCLS automatically turns the request over to ILL. This has resulted in an increase of 14% to the document delivery fill rate from November 1999 to June 2001. This process allows OCLS to shift acquisitions commitments from individual subscriptions to new electronic resources with wider full text availability.

With the advent and growth of easily accessible virtual libraries for all patrons, collection development practices among distance learning and traditional librarians are becoming more similar. However, differences in some collection philosophies between the two groups are still evident. Pamela Grudzien, Head of Collection Development at CMU, in an interview on February 6, 2002, spoke at length on some significant differences she has noted in the selection behaviors of the libraries' subject bibliographers and the OCLS librarians who funnel all requests for electronic purchases through her. Grudzien stated that a significant difference between the two groups of librarians is in how they respond in their discussions about new electronic products on the libraries' collection development electronic list. The OCLS librarians are much more like public librarians in that they look at a new electronic product in terms of how the distance learning clientele will be able to use it whereas the subject bibliographers think more in terms of how they will instruct students to use the product. OCLS librarians often advocate for a new online resource because it will answer the needs of assignments in particular courses while the subject bibliographers think more in terms of the database being useful for a discipline and being desired by faculty in that discipline or needed for accreditation of an academic program.

Grudzien also stated that OCLS librarians become frustrated quickly at the slow speed of the process. They chafe at the amount of time it takes to set up and run trials and the time it can take to make decisions to start a new subscription. The distance learning students, who are working adults whose average age is 37, have more time-sensitive demands and the librarians feel a strong urgency to answer their needs. Most of the faculty who teach in the distance learning programs at CMU are adjunct and rarely take the role in collection development that their full-time campus counterparts do. Part of the role of the subject bibliographers at CMU is to maintain contact with the departments for whom they make selections, so collection development in the libraries is determined to a degree by the teaching faculty. OCLS is often able to make much quicker decisions to add a new online resource or to discontinue one because the librarians do not rely on anyone outside the department for guidance in these decisions.

In 2001, the OCLS librarians made two significant decisions in regard to electronic databases. In one case, they decided to drop the full text subscription to a business database. Although the journal coverage was substantial and a large percentage of the periodicals were not owned by CMU, it was a very expensive product that was not getting high use among the students despite a continued effort of marketing on the part of the OCLS librarians. When the new subscription price revealed an increase of over $10,000 per year for the full text version, the OCLS librarians decided to drop it with little discussion and no outside consultation.

At about the same time, the OCLS librarians decided to subscribe to the E*Subscribe full text database of ERIC documents. OCLS had been looking at this product from its inception to answer the growing problem of students who could not locate microfiche reader/printers in local libraries to read the ERIC documents that were reproduced on microfiche and sent to them. The problem was a particular issue for education students outside the U.S., who had to wait a substantial period of time to receive the microfiche through the mail and then could not find machines to print out the reports. The challenges for some of these students had become so daunting that they had begun a campaign of complaints against OCLS in general that were being sent to the administrators of the distance learning programs on a regular basis. As soon as this database was priced in a way that OCLS could afford it, a subscription was set up and education students were advised of its availability immediately. The education subject bibliographer had also been looking very closely at this product for the main library, but as of the current time, had not made a decision to subscribe because there was no apparent support for it from the education faculty at the university.

CONCLUSION

In the era of primarily print-based materials in libraries, collection development was not a large part of the work of distance learning librarians. Their main impetus was to get the material already in the institutions' collections out to remote students. The most prominent impact they had on libraries' collections was in adding multiple copies to mail to remote students or to be housed in sites near where the remote classes were being taught. As library materials became available electronically, distance learning library services worked to find ways to make these available to the distance learning students. Early efforts were difficult because of the challenges of setting students up with accounts to dial into online systems or the costs of dialing in long distance for many students. The introduction of the World Wide Web as a widespread tool for the dissemination of information in our society has revolutionized the ability to bring library collections to the remote user in a place of his or her convenience 24 hours a day and seven days a week. It has also changed the role that distance learning librarians play in collection development in their libraries. As advocates for the distance learners, the distance learning librarians often shape the priorities in libraries of where to spend the money for electronic resources. In addition, with their own web sites, which are their own avenues of dissemination, distance learning library services can create virtual libraries tailored to their students without having to depend entirely on institutional purchases.

REFERENCES

Angel, M. R., and C. Budnick. 1986. Collection development and acquisitions for service to off-campus students. *Library Acquisitions: Practice and Theory* 10: 13-24.

Association of College and Research Libraries (ACRL). 2000. *Guidelines for distance learning library services*, [http://www.ala.org/acrl/guides/distlrng.html], accessed on 2/7/02.

Campbell, J. O. 1988. Collection development for the library service to external students at the University of Queensland. *Library Acquisitions: Practice and Theory* 12: 269-279.

Casey, A. M., and M. Cachero. 1998. *Off-campus library services director.* 3rd ed. Mount Pleasant: Central Michigan University.

Cusripituck, S., and S. Puttapithakporn. 1988. Collection development and acquisitions for library services to students of Sukhothai Thammathirat Open University. *Library Acquisitions: Practice and Theory* 12: 303-311.

Day, R. and J. Angus. 1986. Off-campus acquisitions at Deakin University Library. *Library Acquisitions: Practice and Theory* 10: 33-42.

Garrett, M. (1988). Going to the head of the class: The development and implementation of an instructional materials support collection. In *The Off-Campus Library Services Conference Proceedings*, edited by B. Lessin. Mount Pleasant: Central Michigan University.

Heilig, J. 2001. E-global library: The academic campus library meets the Internet. *Searcher* 9 (6): 34-43.

Holleman, C. 1998. From Field of Dreams to the Godfather: Collection Development Today. *Against the Grain* 10 (2): 1.

Johnson, J. S. 1987. Collection development for off-campus library services. *Library Acquisitions: Practice and Theory* 11: 75-84.

Kanjilal, U. 1998. *Digital libraries for distance learners: Prospects for India.* Paper presented at the International Conference on New Missions of Academic Libraries in the 21st Century, [http://www.lib.pku.edu.cn/98conf/proceedings.htm], accessed February 7, 2002.

Kanjilal, U., and S. M. Tripathi. 1995. Collection development: Planning for IGNOU library system. *Library Acquisitions: Practice and Theory* 19: 83-95.

Kelly, G. 1987. The development of acquisitions and collection services for off-campus students in northeastern Ontario: An important library collection development issue or merely an issue of a more efficient materials handling and delivery system? *Library Acquisitions: Practice and Theory* 11: 47-66.

McKnight, S. 1998. Library services to off-campus students–an Australian perspective. In *Libraries without walls 2: The delivery of library services to distant users* edited by P. Brophy, S. Fisher, and Z. Clarke, [http://www.deakin.edu.au/library/lww6.html], accessed February 7, 2002.

Murphy, M., and K. Rupp-Serrano. 1999. Interlibrary loan and document delivery: Lessons to be learned. *Journal of Library Administration* 28: 15-24.

Peterman, T. W., and G. A. Schultis. 1993. Providing library support for distance learning: Acquisitions issues. In *The Sixth Off-Campus Library Services Conference Proceedings*, edited by C. J. Jacob. Mount Pleasant: Central Michigan University.

Pettingill, A. H. 1998. Off-campus library resources: Collection development for distance education and its impact on overall library collection goals. In *The Eighth Off-Campus Library Services Conference Proceedings*, edited by S. Thomas and M. Jones. Mount Pleasant: Central Michigan University.

Power, C. J. 1992. The selection and funding of CD-ROMs for the extended-campus. *Collection Development* 16 (3): 1-12.

Ruddy, M. 1988. Infotrac and the Business Collection: A dynamic duo for off-campus programs. In *The Off-Campus Library Services Conference Proceedings*, edited by B. Lessin. Mount Pleasant: Central Michigan University.

Schmude, K. G. and R. B. Luxton. 1986. Acquisitions for distance education: An Australian experience. *Library Acquisitions: Practice and Theory* 10: 25-31.

Silveria, J. B., and Leonard, B. G. 1996. The balancing act: Collection development in support of remote users in an extended campus setting. *Collection Management* 21 (3/4): 139-151.

Whitehead, M. 1987. Collection development for distance education at the University of British Columbia Library. *Library Acquisitions: Practice and Theory* 11:67-74.

Wijesinghe, M. N. 1988. Provision of library resources for Open University students in Sri Lanka. *Library Acquisitions: Practice and Theory* 12:297-302.

Willemse, J. 1986. An acquisitions policy to promote distance teaching at the University of South Africa. *Library Acquisitions: Practice and Theory* 10:43-53.

Williams, E. W. 1986. Distant libraries for distance education in the South Pacific. *Library Acquisitions: Practice and Theory* 10:55-66.

Zietlow, R., and J. Kragness. 1993. Implementing a virtual library for off-campus students. In *The Sixth Off-Campus Library Services Conference Proceedings*, edited by C. J. Jacob. Mount Pleasant: Central Michigan University.

An Uncertain Trumpet:
Developing Archival and Special Collections in the Electronic Era

William J. Crowe

SUMMARY. In the era of electronic information, it is important that the leaders in the larger community connect, or reconnect, with the leaders of all of the specialties that fall within the archives, rare books, and manuscript sector. *[Article copies available for a fee from The Haworth Document Delivery Service: 1-800-HAWORTH. E-mail address: <getinfo@haworth pressinc.com> Website: <http://www.HaworthPress.com> © 2002 by The Haworth Press, Inc. All rights reserved.]*

KEYWORDS. Electronic information, electronic era, special collections

This contribution to the literature is, in truth, rumination. It reflects the views of a librarian who has placed himself, in late career, in the archival and special collections community at the beginning of the new century. The uncertainty about the call of the trumpet, then, may be as much in the author's mind as in the times!

Is the trumpet signaling alarm or is it a call to action? The call–in either case–is of course being issued by scholars and others in our society who traditionally have been concerned with the capture and transmission of recorded knowledge, especially original records of human experience. How should that call be heard and acted upon in the library

---

William J. Crowe is Spencer Librarian, University of Kansas, Lawrence, KS 66045-17616.

[Haworth co-indexing entry note]: "An Uncertain Trumpet: Developing Archival and Special Collections in the Electronic Era." Crowe, William J. Co-published simultaneously in *Journal of Library Administration* (The Haworth Information Press, an imprint of The Haworth Press, Inc.) Vol. 36, No. 3, 2002, pp. 73-80; and: *Electronic Resources and Collection Development* (ed: Sul H. Lee) The Haworth Information Press, an imprint of The Haworth Press, Inc., 2002, pp. 73-80. Single or multiple copies of this article are available for a fee from The Haworth Document Delivery Service [1-800-HAWORTH, 9:00 a.m. - 5:00 p.m. (EST). E-mail address: getinfo@haworthpressinc.com].

community, notably in that part of the community concerned with archives and rare books and manuscripts?

The perspective of the author is that of a long time general library administrator whose professional specialty was in acquisitions, cataloging, and systems, with a strong commitment to work for improved collaboration and cooperation among libraries and between libraries and other entities, such as archives and museums, that share responsibility for the capture, organization and transmission of the cultural record. This perspective is also affected by the author's research interest in the study of leadership and the shaping of change in American libraries during the 20th century.

From this vantage, one can ruminate, with uncertainty to be sure, but also with some conviction, enough to be prepared to *suggest* something of where we may be headed . . . what the nature of the call is and how we in the archival and special collections community, in concert with our colleagues from other sectors, should respond. The core observation may be too obvious: it is imperative that the leaders in the larger library community connect, or reconnect, with the leaders of all of the specialties that fall within the archives, rare books, and manuscripts sector. It is equally important that the leaders and practitioners in the archival and special collections communities redouble *their* efforts to get to know *each other* better.

Connecting these communities with the larger body of general library staff also is necessary to close a gap in understanding that may not have been so apparent one or two generations ago. Consider the paths by which many men (almost always men) rose to positions of leadership in the research libraries of a half-century ago. They often were "bookmen," builders of collections and lovers and buyers of books and manuscripts, who were at ease in the homes of bibliophiles and the shops of booksellers. This was very much the case in some of the libraries with which the author has been associated: Cecil Byrd at Indiana and Robert Vosper at Kansas. . . . These library leaders and others like them needed no introduction to the rare book, manuscripts or archival collections and many of the general library staff were conversant with many of the basic issues of special, as well as general, collections because of the nature of professional education and the nature of scholarly communication of the times.

Consider how many of the leaders in the university research library community in North America today might claim such knowledge. Consider also how many leaders in the archival and special collections communities converse on a regular basis with senior university libraries administration or how many rank and file manuscripts and rare books librarians and archivists regularly meet with their colleagues from other library departments.

The climate for re-engagement is very promising, if only because we are rediscovering in the age of the web and of digital library planning, but also of such innovations in teaching and research as promotion of "public history," that the distinctive strengths of our great libraries are once again understood to be very much in their special and archival collections. The development of many a great open stacks collection has been hard hit in most university libraries by three decades of the flight of money to the serial budget and, in the last dozen years, by the need to acquire access to electronic information.

But the climate for change in archival and special collections also is being driven by a growing realization that the changes in scholarly communication that the research library community seeks to promote demand that successful planning be clear about the end goal. That end is not only the containment of current costs, but truly to sustain the indispensable link that libraries always have called their own: the collecting, authenticating, and archiving the record of scholarship. Only with this end kept always in view can efforts at change enable succeeding generations to test and sift, to challenge and endorse, to celebrate and dismiss what has gone before.

In their often intensive engagement with scholars and students, the archivist (consider the numerical data manager and geo-spatial specialist in this group) and the special collections librarian have an opportunity, hour by hour, directly and intimately, to learn about and often to influence the work of the current and the next generation of creators of knowledge. Much of the work of our general collections library staff has of necessity been tuned to the creation of tools and techniques that enable the learner to proceed to the maximum degree (24/7!) without the need for close personal interaction with a member of the staff.

Can we assert now that we know our clients as our predecessors may have known their readers? Have we been led to be so efficient that we encounter clients only at the circulation desk, in a mass instruction session, or during an occasional query (conveyed electronically) to a bibliographer or reference librarian who has little time to develop or sustain personal contact beyond the moment?

If we have redeployed staff because of such efficiencies to reach out, to leave the desk, to engage scholars and students in other ways, we may help them to explore our traditional collections, to call on records of human experience, to teach old verities, and to explore new meanings. Working with a professor who understands that teaching students to look into the records of past pandemics–from the Black Plague, to the Yellow Fever outbreaks of not too many decades ago, the Spanish Influenza, tuberculosis, and the polio epidemics of the days before Salk–can help them understand the new challenges of AIDS and illness caused by hazardous materials. Literature and philosophy, history and religion, records of scientists and professionals of earlier times of course can yield much fresh understanding!

How can we teach and learn about the geo-politics of the post-Cold War era without access to the best, meaning original, record of the history of other cultures, of encounters between and among peoples, of their political, religious, and economic values? Can we discover something of the Afghan wars and the seeds of racial conflicts in Africa by reading the books for boys of late Victorian Britain? Can the diary of a sea captain from New England help us understand the shared responsibility of North and South in the United States for the evils of the slave trade? Can the household accounts and diaries of women on the Great Plains of the United States in the mid-19th century help us understand the political culture of the American heartland? . . . and we cannot overlook the archives of sound and images in motion, of numeric and spatial data, too of course.

It is important to be alert to what *is* being done to answer the call, even as we seek out issues that yet need attention. Actions being taken in the general research library community and in the archival and special collections communities are very encouraging.

Among the most important of these initiatives are those of the Association of Research Libraries, of the Council on Library and Information Resources, the Research Libraries Group, OCLC Online Computer Library Center, and the U.S. federal government.

The revival of interest in archival and special collections among leaders in the Association of Research Libraries is traceable to the work of the Research Collections Committee, led by Joe Hewitt, of the University of North Carolina at Chapel Hill, in the late 1990s. That committee's comprehensive 1998 survey of the state of special collections held among the ARL member libraries was published in 2001. This work was meant also to advance the discussions held during the May 1999 semiannual meeting of the ARL, held under the leadership of Betty Bengtson at Kansas City, Missouri, and Lawrence, Kansas, for which the meeting theme was the future of special collections in the digital age. The committee's work led to an unprecedented gathering at Brown University, in June 2001, of the directors of many ARL member libraries and the heads of many special collections units. That meeting's agenda was to advise on the shaping of a North American agenda, whose work is now well advanced.

The Council on Library and Information Resources, which, with its antecedent bodies, long has shown interest in and support for so many advances in the field, has in this sphere also helped lead the way. The Council's Task Force on the Artifact in Library Collections, whose report, *The Evidence in Hand . . .* , was issued in 2001, adds substantial weight to the dialogue about the future of these collections from the perspective of the scholarly community.

The work of the U.S federal government, in particular in recent years of the National Endowment for the Humanities and the Institute for Museum and Library Services, has opened many opportunities for collaboration among libraries, archives and museums, and so given many librarians, curators, and archivists opportunities to learn about each other in ways that lead often to collaborative ventures.

There have been heartening signs of productive collaboration between the Research Libraries Group and OCLC Online Computer Library Center, especially to promote sharing of work to develop standards with others and promote adherence to standards in such important work as digitization and creation of meta data. This collaboration is vital to the successful bridging of communities of interest in North America and worldwide.

Still, what is lacking or not sufficiently advanced in development?

In the end, the greatest need is for more action to engage larger numbers of practitioners in the field with each other and with librarians who practice in other sectors of the library. The potential value of exchanges of perspectives can help all comprehend the challenges we face collectively. The great strengths of the archivist or manuscripts librarian, for example, in applying different principles to the organization of bodies of often truly unique documents itself can be eye opening for those among us whose careers have been spent dealing with published material. Think of the insights that may be had for librarians struggling to identify and provide access to the plethora of unique digital, web-based resources that are proliferating around the world. If for no other reason than to be reminded that there are fellow information professionals whose life's work has been productively spent dealing successfully with very similar challenges. Archivists and manuscripts librarians do not accept defeat in the face of often overwhelming bodies of disparate material, which is the same spirit that should animate the work of those who work with the newer forms of electronic information.

Yet another example of how the larger group of librarians may profit from dialogue with their colleagues in the archival realms is to become more familiar with the pioneering work being done by archivists, working closely with leaders in information technology, to grapple with our responsibilities to capture the "documentary record" when that record is now often found only in electronic form. Archivists have faced the discontinuation of old, paper-based systems in many organizations, indeed the seeming scattering of data files that now may constitute, for example, the records of admissions, registration, enrollment, and academic progress of all of a university's students. There are many lessons here for those of us who are faced with the capture of electronic data appearing in so many forms and created for so many disparate purposes.

Librarians also may profit from exposure to some of the other time-tested practices of archivists, for example, their ability to exercise rigorous appraisal of the value of records for retention and often to discard ruthlessly. This process may be likened to the practice of skilled bibliographers who cull publishers' offerings to select rigorously the traditional books and journals to be added to collections, but the approach may be worth close examination as more librarians encounter such tasks as the need to select larger and larger numbers of items for removal to remote storage. Archivists and librarians who are to succeed cannot be faint of heart in decision-making about collection development or document appraisal!

Of most interest to a general collections librarian about the experience of archivists and rare book and special collections librarians may be the survival of the reference interview, that often extended dialogue that regularly occurs between a student or scholar-reader and archivist or rare book or manuscript librarian. The persistence of the deep relationships that can develop as the information professional engages the researcher in often very personal ways offers remarkable opportunities for the library as a whole to gain insight into the development of new methods of research and new avenues being opened, or of old methods and avenues being revived and reopened! These exchanges, which often first bring to light for the library the attributes of interdisciplinary work being done in the humanities and social sciences (and in some areas of the sciences, too) offer a chance for the library to influence the thinking of scholars about how they communicate their research, how they and their colleagues teach, and how they can better come to understand their responsibility to sustain the building of the scholarly record.

The rising generation of scholars may come to see the archivist or rare books librarian as one of the few professional colleagues outside her or his specialty community who can offer a sounding board, as well as all of the "knowledge navigation" skills so necessary to plumb many a special collection or archive. Do the leaders of our great libraries understand that remaining within their walls is a lively vestige of the kind of personal interaction of which some older scholars and librarians speak wistfully? Have we listened to our colleagues here? Have we taken care to provide them with the latest and best information about developments in scholarly communication being advanced by the library community and some scholarly societies?

Such exchanges are of course not unique to the archives or rare books reading room! But it may well be the case that in these settings there will be more consistent opportunities for the library community to engage scholars in their formative years . . . to plant and nurture ideas, to cajole on occasion, and to celebrate, and at times, gently, to admonish . . . appealing to the best traditions of scholarship and of these specialties within our professions . . . and so better to connect generations of scholars with each other.

I have come to better understand why many archivists and rare book and manuscript librarians see themselves as at once privileged not because of their sometime palatial appearing quarters and their close connections with the unusual and "special," but because they have the opportunity on an everyday basis to get to know many of their clients in a setting that naturally encourages the development of deeper relationships than has come often to be the case for librarians who practice in many areas of the research library community.

Let us enlist our special collections and archivist colleagues. In that, let all of *us* sound a trumpet with some certainty in the cause of promoting wondrous digitization projects based in special collections and to expose students and faculty–and the general public–anew to the rewards of discovery in primary sources, and not to preserve these core collections out of sentiment or nostalgia of halcyon days long past.

The call must also come out of a conviction that the wider library community can profit from a better understanding of many of the time tested approaches used in special collections to capture and organize the record of human experience and from the intelligence that these information professionals can offer to the larger community about the paths being followed by many promising researchers. And it may be that with the informed help of these information professionals that those researchers can themselves be helped to hear the call . . . to reform and recapture the core elements of scholarly communication.

BIBLIOGRAPHY

Association of Research Libraries. "A Proposed ARL Action Agenda for Special Collections," Available online at *http://www.arl.org/special/action.html*.

Philip C. Bantin, "Developing a Strategy for Managing Electronic Records: The Findings of the Indiana University Electronic Records Project," *American Archivist* 61 (1998): 337-338.

Robert L. Byrd, " 'One Day . . . It Will Be Otherwise' Changing the Reputation and Reality of Special Collections," Available online at *http://www.arl.org/special/byrd.html*.

The Evidence in Hand: Report of the Task Force on the Artifact in Library Collections (Washington: Council on Library and Information Resources, 2001).

Jeffrey Peter Hart, *Smiling Through Cultural Catastrophe* (New Haven: Yale University Press, 2001).

Tom Hyry, review of *The Archival Image: Collected Essays*, by Eric Ketelaar, and *The Concept of Record: Report from the Second Stockholm Conference on Archival Science and the Concept of Record*, published by the Swedish National Archives, *American Archivist* 62:170-173.

Steven Lubar, "Information Culture and the Archival Record," *American Archivist* 62 (1999): 10-22.

Henri Jean Martin, *The History and Power of Writing* (Chicago: University of Chicago Press, 1994).

Thomas E. Nisonger, issue ed. "Collection Development in an Electronic Environment," *Library Trends* 48 (Spring 2000).

Carole L. Palmer and Laura J. Neumann, "The Information Work of Interdisciplinary Humanities Scholars: Exploration and Translation," *Library Quarterly* 72 (2002): 85-117.

Special Collections in ARL Libraries: Results of the 1998 Survey sponsored by the ARL Research Collections Committee (Washington: Association of Research Libraries, 2001).

Stephen C. Wagner, "Integrated Archives and Records Management Programs at Professional Membership Associations: A Case Study and a Model," *American Archivist* 62 (1999): 95-129.

The ARL Scholars Portal Initiative

Mary E. Jackson

SUMMARY. This article describes a new initiative of the Association of Research Libraries (ARL)–the Scholars Portal Initiative. Background, current activities, and next steps of the Project will be discussed.

KEYWORDS. Association of Research Libraries (ARL), Scholars Portal Initiative, Scholars Portal Working Group

INTRODUCTION

It is an honor being asked to give a paper at this conference. I would like to thank Dean Sul Lee and his colleagues at the University of Oklahoma Libraries for inviting me and for making this year's conference yet another success.

It's my pleasure to spend a few minutes describing a new initiative of the Association of Research Libraries (ARL)–the Scholars Portal Initiative. I'll begin by describing the Scholars Portal Project–background, current activities, and next steps of the Project. I will highlight some of the other activities within the larger initiative and will briefly address how portal activities in general will facilitate access to information resources for users of research libraries.

Mary E. Jackson is Senior Program Officer for Access Services, Association of Research Libraries, Washington, DC 20036.

[Haworth co-indexing entry note]: "The ARL Scholars Portal Initiative." Jackson, Mary E. Co-published simultaneously in *Journal of Library Administration* (The Haworth Information Press, an imprint of The Haworth Press, Inc.) Vol. 36, No. 3, 2002, pp. 81-91; and: *Electronic Resources and Collection Development* (ed: Sul H. Lee) The Haworth Information Press, an imprint of The Haworth Press, Inc., 2002, pp. 81-91.

A BRIEF LOOK BACK

The ARL-OCLC Strategic Issues Forum, held in Keystone, Colorado in September 1999 was memorable for two reasons: the development of the Keystone Principles[1] and the germination of the concept that would become known as the Scholars Portal. Participants at the Strategic Issues Forum agreed that libraries were in danger of abandoning their constituencies to commercial information services in the Web environment. The library Web presence was not (and is still not) an acceptable general entry point to the larger range of Web resources. Participants concluded that it was necessary to increase the research library presence on the Web by advancing the concept of a "library.org."

Jerry Campbell, Chief Information Officer and Dean of University Libraries, University of Southern California, advanced that idea in his May 2000 White Paper prepared for discussion by the ARL membership at their May 2000 meeting. Campbell's paper asked the ARL membership to consider what role the Association should play in portal development for the scholarly community.[2] He suggested that ARL seriously pursue the feasibility of developing a "library.org" Web presence. He argued for a collaborative partnership approach, and asserted that research librarians can create a Scholars Portal better than anyone else. Dr. Campbell was the first to articulate some of the key features and functionality of such a portal. He suggested that the portal should include high quality content, be based on standards, search across multiple and disparate databases, offer a variety of supporting tools, offer enhanced supporting services such as digital reference, and have the capability of integrating electronic thesauri. Dr. Campbell asserted that this portal was "the place to start for anyone seeking academically sound information."

EXPANDING THE CONCEPT

Sarah Thomas, University Librarian, Cornell University Libraries, built on Campbell's thesis in her article "Abundance, Attention, and Access: of Portals and Catalogs," which was published in the October 2000 issue of *ARL Biomonthly Report*.[3] Thomas was one of the first to assert that the emphasis should be on the identification of many new resources of value to the scholar and researcher, rather than on the cataloging of only a few, relatively speaking, new items. She coined a new word: "portalog."

THE ARL SCHOLARS PORTAL WORKING GROUP

In early 2000 the ARL Board of Directors established a small working group to think through and recommend a practical vision for a Scholars Portal and a possible ARL role in developing such a proposal. Jerry Campbell was appointed Chair of the ARL Scholars Portal Working Group.[4] Early in its deliberations, the Working Group established two cornerstone principles. First, access to disparate electronic resources and services can be improved through integration, both within a single institution and among multiple institutions. Second, efforts to effect such integration should leverage work already being carried out in ARL libraries rather than requiring new work of those libraries.

THE SCHOLARS PORTAL VISION

The Scholars Portal vision supports at least five key features. First, users will be able to discover resources through the discovery tool. Users will be able to capture content or information about content through the use of harvesting and delivery tools. Third, users will be able to manipulate content by the use of text-processing and citation-management tools. Fourth, users will be able to distribute content via contribution and publication tools. Finally, users will be able to consult with others in the electronic scholarly communities via access to virtual reference services or lists and chat services.

"A SUPER DISCOVERY TOOL"

Recognizing that the range of features and services will be required to realize the vision articulated by the Scholars Portal Working Group, the Working Group agreed that the cross-platform searching was the critical first step. The Working Group identified a number of diverse targets for searching. They include the local online catalog and other library's online catalogs, vetted Web sites, locally licensed full-text and abstracting and indexing databases, public domain or publicly accessible abstracting and indexing services, finding aids for special collections and archives, and digitized material owned locally or by another library, museum, or archive. Recognizing that the Scholars Portal should offer a range of supporting services and tools, the Working Group narrowed its focus to the development of specifications (conceptual, functional, and technical) for a "super discovery tool" with the understanding that the other functions would not be possible without a robust discovery tool.

At first the Working Group assumed that such a tool did not exist, but the Working Group also recognized that ARL, as an organization, would not be in a position to develop the tool itself. The Working Group anticipated contracting with a software developer to build the tool, but wanted to undertake an environmental scan of portal products before it embarked down a long developmental path.

ENVIRONMENTAL SCAN

During spring 2001, the Working Group made a decision not to issue a formal Request for Proposal (RFP) or Request for Information (RFI) as it was felt that the development, issuance, and review of responses to an RFP or RFI would slow down the ambitious timeline set by the Working Group. Instead, the Working Group developed a list of key features it felt was required or highly desirable in the discovery tool of a portal, and included some other features of a portal. That list, included as Appendix A, was used in the Working Group's environmental scan, and a list of features was enhanced during the several months of the environmental scan. But, the list has not been updated since it was completed in May 2001.

During these early discussions, the Working Group undertook an environment scan and identified over 40 potential portal products. Having identified a core list of key features of the discovery tool, such as the ability to search library catalogs and the free Web, the list of products was narrowed considerably. Many portal products were aimed at organizing internal records and/or searching only Web resources. The Working Group was also looking for a company that was ready and willing to engage in a project rather than an organization wanting to develop or co-develop a product. Several potential collaborators were dismissed because the Working Group felt that they were not in a position to work in a collaborative environment with research libraries or were overextended in their current marketplace.

ADVANCING THE PROJECT: SEEKING BOARD APPROVAL

In late spring 2001 the Working Group met with several companies and organizations to learn more about their products and their readiness to work in a collaborative project with ARL member institutions. The Working Group selected one company and made a recommendation to the ARL Board of Directors. At its July 2001 meeting, the ARL Board supported the Working Group's recommendation to begin "collaborative exploration" with that vendor that would lead to a project.

The preferred vendor was selected for several reasons.[5] First the Working Group believed its product included many of the key features identified by the Working Group. Also important in the selection was the readiness and experience of the vendor to collaborate on advancing the priorities of the project.

WHY THE NAME SCHOLARS PORTAL?

Jerry Campbell's early use of the name "Scholars Portal" has "stuck," even though many argue that it is not accurate. The portal is not just for faculty or researchers. In fact, the Working Group agreed that the initial focus would be the undergraduate student, whom some argue is the future researcher. Portal is equally inaccurate as the vision is not just a gateway or path to institutional resources. Sarah Thomas suggested that a portal is the "entry point to the Web."[6]

WHAT IS THE GOAL OF THE SCHOLARS PORTAL PROJECT?

The Scholars Portal Project seeks to provide tools for an academic community to have a single point of access on the Web to find high-quality information resources and, to the greatest extent possible, to deliver the information and related services directly to the user's desktop. The Working Group envisions the construction of a suite of Web-based services that will connect the higher education community as directly as possible with quality information resources that contribute to the teaching and learning process and that advance research.

The Project also seeks to leverage existing efforts underway in research libraries. The Working Group expects that the project participants will work with their academic colleagues to help curate and shape the content.

The Scholars Portal Project is a three-year collaborative effort. A self-selected group of ARL member libraries will implement the software and test the existing product. Project Participants will reach consensus on additional functionality needed in the existing product to realize the Scholars Portal vision. The vendor is contributing development resources to build that additional functionality.

The first emphasis of the Scholars Portal Project is on cross-domain searching and the aggregation and integration of search results from a wide range of resources. Future activities will include linkage to online learning environments and course management products, the introduction of digital reference services, and links to other supporting services.

THE CURRENT STATUS

The Working Group is very, very, very close to signing a contract and issuing a press release. We have begun securing commitments from ARL members to participate in the Scholars Portal Project. [As of May, 2002, seven ARL member institutions had agreed to participate as Initial Project Participants.]

NOT THE ONLY GAME IN TOWN

The collaboration with one vendor aims to demonstrate the viability of the Scholars Portal vision with one vendor's products. Even as the Scholars Portal Project is launched, other ARL members are working on similar projects with other vendors. The collaboration with one vendor is *not* an ARL endorsement of that vendor or its products.

ARL'S ROLE: MOVING FROM SCHOLARS PORTAL PROJECT TO SCHOLARS PORTAL INITIATIVE

The libraries participating in the Scholars Portal Project sought and received ARL's ongoing involvement because they believe that this will spur all vendors to work even harder to create products that serve the needs of research library communities. I am serving as part-time Project Manager for the Project and will continue to monitor portal software applications generally. ARL plans to establish an Implementers Group for vendors of portal products to discuss such issues as needed standards and interoperability between portal products and other software tools.

Another activity within the larger initiative is the tracking of implementations in ARL member libraries. In February 2002, ARL surveyed its members on the state of portal implementations. We will disseminate the results of that survey to the larger library community. We are planning a workshop or conference for fall to highlight how research libraries are implementing portal tools. Finally, ARL will continue to report on the experiences to the library community.

OUTSTANDING QUESTIONS

A number of questions have been raised about the Scholars Portal Project and ARL's role in that project. Let me address only a few.

First, why did ARL select only one vendor as a partner? Let me correct that question and note that it was the Working Group, and not the association or ARL staff, that selected the vendor. The Working Group felt that by choosing a single vendor it would encourage other vendors to enter the marketplace with competitive tools to advance portal functionality. As many of you know, ARL used a different model to advance ILL functionality–describing features and requirements research libraries needed in ILL products and encouraging vendors to go off and build products that met our needs. Even after a decade of encouragement, we realized only modest success with that model. So, we are trying a different model, and will see if this approach is more successful.

Another question asked is whether the Working Group has selected the right business model. It's important to note that the Scholars Portal Project participants are paying all project expenses, including my role as part-time Project Manager. No ARL dues are earmarked for the Project. For now, this is a workable business model.

Finally, the Working Group has already been asked if its vision is correct. That is a question that we will be able to answer at the end of the project. It's a bit premature to speculate any response at this point.

CONCLUSION

Like other portal initiatives, the Scholars Portal Project seeks the development of a suite of Web-based tools and supporting services that will connect the higher education community as directly as possible with high quality information. We hope these tools and services will permit users to perform integrated searches, access a range of high quality information, and have seamless access to digital reference and interlibrary loan/document delivery services. The Working Group sees real potential for strong collaboration among Collection Managers and others who select Web resources and the exposing of locally digitized collections to the wider research community. Finally, we hope that Project participants will be able to obtain aggregated usage data on the range of information resources targeted and in ways that have not been possible to this point.

Thank you again for inviting me. I welcome your questions and comments.

NOTES

1. The Keystone Principles. Available at: <http://www.arl.org/training/keystone.html>.

2. Jerry D. Campbell, "The Case for Creating a Scholars Portal to the Web: A White Paper," Available at: <http://www.arl.org/newsltr/211/portal.html>.

3. Sarah Thomas, "Abundance, Attention, and Access: of Portals and Catalogs," Available at: <http://www.arl.org/newsltr/212/portal.html>.

4. See http://www.arl.org/access/scholarsportal/ for a list of current members of the ARL Scholars Portal Working Group.

5. At the time of the conference the name of the vendor was not public. Subsequently, ARL issued a press release announcing Fretwell-Downing, Inc. as the partner in the Scholars Portal Project. Press release available at: <http://www.arl.org/arl/pr/scholars_portal.html>.

6. Sarah Thomas, "The Catalog as Portal to the Internet," (Contributed to the Library of Congress's Bicentennial Conference on Bibliographic Control for the New Millennium, 15-17 November 2000). The full text of the paper is available at: <http://www.arl.org/arl/pr/scholars_portal.html>.

APPENDIX A

Features and Functionality in Portals

A Working List developed by the
ARL Scholars Portal Working Group
Spring, 2001

This outline of features and functionality was developed to aid the ARL Scholars Portal Working Group in its environmental scan of potential portal products during the spring of 2001. Because the Working Group was focused on the discovery tool, the list reflects a bias toward features found in search tools. The list was not designed to be comprehensive, but represents the features and functionality Working Group members articulated as their highest priority. In spring 2001, the Working Group was not aware of any readably available list of portal features or functional requirements, so the Working Group developed this list as an aid in their understanding existing products. The Working Group was and is aware that the understandings of features a portal should include will evolve over time. This list represents the views of the ARL Scholars Portal Working group as of June 2001; it has not been kept up to date. If the Working Group were to develop such a list today, the features and functionality are likely to differ.

1. **General Information**
   - What is the name and version number of the product(s)?
   - Does the company have additional portal-related products?

2. **Fall 2001 Pilot**
   - Does the company have an existing product to test this fall?
   - Is the prototype customizable?

3. **Patron Authentication**
   - Does the product support 3M's SIP?
   - Does the product support NCIP?
   - Does the product support LDAP?
   - Does the product support Kerberos?
   - Does the product support PKI?
   - Does the product provide a proprietary authentication system?
   - Does the product support rights management tracking?
   - Does the product provide a one-step login to remote databases?
   - Does the product authorize users database by database?

4. **User Interface**
   - Does the product have a clean design?
   - Is the User Interface customizable?

APPENDIX A (continued)

- Can the user personalize/refine/modify search and search results?
- Does the product include help screens?
- Does the product include an online tutorial?
- Can a participant integrate the "Scholars Portal" logo into the local Web pages?

5. Search Engine
- Does the product include a thesaurus? If so, which one(s)?
- Is the thesaurus static or dynamic?
- Can the product map the thesaurus vocabulary across different controlled vocabularies?
- Does the product include a crosswalk among different classification schemes?
- Can the search screen be personalized by database?
- Does the product search metadata of different types of resource formats, including multimedia?
- Can the vendor host content in a centralized database?
- Can the product search across distributed databases?
- Can the product be configured to limit a search to a specific content provider or database?
- Does the product provide access to the native search mode for advanced users?
- Does the product support keyword searching?
- Does the product support full-text indexing of digital text resources?
- Does the product support Open URL?
- Does the product support Open Archives Metadata Harvesting Protocol?
- Does the product handle foreign languages?
- Does the product handle non-Roman scripts?
- Does the product support Z39.50 searching?
- Does the product support HTTP searches of Web resources?
- What type of record structure does the product support?
  - MARC
  - EAD
  - Dublin Core
  - GILS
  - CIMI
  - RDF
- Can the product harvest all ".edu" sites?
- Can the product access OCLC's WorldCat?
- Can the product access RLG's Union Catalog?
- Does the product include push features regarding new resources?
- Does the product provide the ability to contribute and update resources or sources to be searched?

6. Search Results
- Does the product save searches for use in an alerting service?
- What is the default display of search results?
- Does the product have an ability to present search results in an unbiased manner?

- Does the product merge and dedupe search results?
- Does the product identify the type of material (e.g., citation, full-text resource, Web page)?
- Does the search result display information on the source of the citation?
- Does the product present appropriate delivery options for each search result?
- Does the product identify if an item in a search result is owned locally?
- Can the product sort result sets by subject, target, etc.?
- Does the product present different views of resources: by task, subject, user group, data, service, locally owned/accessible, etc.?
- Does the product point to an appropriate copy?
- Does the product link to the full-text article if locally licensed?

7. Linkages with other Systems
- Does the product have a link to one or more ISO ILL Protocol-compliant messaging systems?
- Does the product have a link to one or more commercial document delivery suppliers?
- Does the product have a link to a 24x7 reference service?

8. Miscellaneous
- What types of usage statistics are provided?
- Is the product installed locally?
- Is the product vendor-hosted, or can it be?

9. Partnership
- Can the company access content from a participant's licensed resources?
- Can the company execute a library's existing license with a content provider?
- What are some examples of existing installations?
- What is the endurance of the company?
- What is the trust of the company as a partner?
- Does the company have corporate resources to deliver current and planned functionality?
- Can the company deliver on its promise?
- What is the role of ARL?
- How many libraries is the company willing to include in the initial pilot?
- How is the product branded?

10. Financial Issues
- Is the product purchased?
- Is the product licensed?
- What is the license fee?
- What is the annual maintenance fee?
- What is the cost to the project participants?
- What is the cost to a library using the product in an operational mode?
- Will the partner be compensated? If so, how?
- Will the product be owned by ARL and/or the participants?
- Who owns the components and enhanced features developed in the partnership?

Think Globally, Act Locally: Electronic Resources and Collection Development

Sarah E. Thomas

SUMMARY. Despite numerous cooperative collection development endeavors, the building of library collections has remained a highly individual and local practice. The physicality of bound volumes has posed a distinct limitation on our ability to share collections, although libraries have made huge strides in recent years. Electronic resources and the ability to digitize our physical holdings offer the potential to redirect our investments in collection building to the creation of a global network that would serve an international community of scholars. By facilitating the creation of discipline-based portals to knowledge resources, librarians can channel their efforts to the benefit of many without sacrificing the quality of local relationships. To accomplish this, libraries need to develop collectively built and managed Web sites that supplant the need for autonomous, selector-created "webliographies" and that greatly expand the number of sources that can be identified and described. Selectors, freed of the individual responsibility to shoulder the increasingly heavy and ultimately unsustainable load of tracking a proliferation of resources in a variety of formats and states of publication, can turn their attention to the capture of more elusive, but important, material; to more detailed evaluation of the use of information resources; toward improvements in the user interface of portals; or toward the transformation of scholarly communication, with

---

Sarah E. Thomas is Carl A. Kroch University Librarian, Cornell University.

[Haworth co-indexing entry note]: "Think Globally, Act Locally: Electronic Resources and Collection Development." Thomas, Sarah E. Co-published simultaneously in *Journal of Library Administration* (The Haworth Information Press, an imprint of The Haworth Press, Inc.) Vol. 36, No. 3, 2002, pp. 93-107; and: *Electronic Resources and Collection Development* (ed: Sul H. Lee) The Haworth Information Press, an imprint of The Haworth Press, Inc., 2002, pp. 93-107. Single or multiple copies of this article are available for a fee from The Haworth Document Delivery Service [1-800-HAWORTH, 9:00 a.m. - 5:00 p.m. (EST). E-mail address: getinfo@haworthpressinc.com].

93

the discipline-based portal serving as a magnet for attracting new forms of scholarly thought and research. *[Article copies available for a fee from The Haworth Document Delivery Service: 1-800-HAWORTH. E-mail address: <getinfo@haworthpressinc.com> Website: <http://www.HaworthPress.com> © 2002 by The Haworth Press, Inc. All rights reserved.]*

KEYWORDS. Electronic resources, collection development, discipline based portals

"My library is down," taunted the computer scientist, speaking to the librarian of his main reference source, Google. This faculty member, an internationally known digital library specialist, claims that he and many of his colleagues meet 80% of their information needs through the open Internet. He spends perhaps 50% of the semester off campus consulting, attending meetings, and at his second home, so the ability to access material online is critical. Like many scientists and engineers, he foresees a declining role for the library over the coming years, as more and more material is available online in an unmediated form. He eyes the space occupied by bookstacks covetously, and not altogether teasingly suggests that his research group might move in to a floor that will become vacant as printed materials become obsolete.

At the opposite end of the spectrum, a noted historian drafting a new book, a study of Sojourner Truth, enters the library when it opens at eight A.M. and departs late at night, moving between her fourth floor study and the Rare and Manuscript Collection, where she consults primary sources and a large collection of anti-slavery pamphlets from the early to mid-nineteenth century. She composes her manuscript on a laptop and makes extensive use of electronic full-text resources, but her bibliography will contain references predominantly to printed materials or handwritten archives. Like many of her humanist colleagues, she possesses considerably higher expectations for the continued value of the library over the coming years. Her fervent wish is for longer opening hours, as well as increased online access to scholarly resources.

Whether they are information scientists or humanists, academicians mirror our culture at large in relation to certain characteristics. They want the convenience of anytime, anyplace service that is increasingly ubiquitous in banking, purchasing, and other customer-oriented operations. In their libraries, they want 24-hour virtual and physical access. They want one-stop shopping and convenience. Increasingly pressed for time, squeezed by mounting professional demands and the shared family responsibilities of dual career couples, they seek efficiencies that enable them to manage their own information needs and enhance their productivity. The LibQual survey conducted through the initiative of the Association of Research Libraries reveals the strong emphasis placed on self-reliance by library users. Libraries have developed an array of innovative services to enable readers to locate and manipulate information on their own. North Carolina State Libraries' MyLibrary, for example, enables the user to create her own gateway to information resources. Other aids to user empowerment are self-help tutorials that explain how to access library resources, electronic reserves, or well-designed Web pages that facilitate intuitive retrieval. Today's scholar and student will often function in a multidisciplinary, multilingual, and cross-institutional environment. For example, Cornell University, Rockefeller University, and the Memorial Sloan Kettering Cancer Center have a tri-lateral agreement in which the three health sciences campuses (including the New York City-based Weill Cornell Medical College) share resources. Cornell's Ithaca campus offers depth in computer science and chemistry that the more narrowly focused health science institutions cannot, and reciprocally, a Cornell graduate student in chemistry can move to one of the New York City partners for more specialized biochemistry training. In such a framework the definition of what is "local" shifts to a more expansive concept than had been possible in an earlier era, the pre-Internet age. The user frequently needs information beyond the boundaries of the host institution's collection. Indeed, where once there were libraries that could supply almost all faculty requests on site, it is inconceivable today that any one organization could aspire to such an aim.

As a consequence of the changing information environment and changing patterns of scholarship and learning, academic users are developing new information behaviors that are important for libraries to monitor and analyze. JSTOR, an online resource providing access to retrospective periodical literature for readers and a collection management tool for libraries, conducted a survey of faculty views on electronic resources and libraries in 2000. Faculty as a whole considered the Internet or World Wide Web as slightly more important for their research than the library catalog, although this was not (yet) the case for humanists. They perceived a declining dependence on libraries as a resource, anticipating a 10% drop over the next five years in those who consider the library "very important."[1]

Another instrument providing insight into the attitudes and expectations of library users is LibQual. Organized by the Association of Research Libraries in conjunction with Texas A&M University Library, this survey of 43 college and research libraries conducted in 2001 examined the minimum, perceived and desired expectations for libraries by library users. At Cornell University the areas with the greatest gaps between the desired and perceived service lay in categories such as "convenient business hours," "enabling me to find information myself 24 hours a day," "full-text delivered electronically to individual users," "complete runs of journals," "a haven for quiet and solitude," and "a library Website enabling me to locate information on my own." Although the Cornell University Library consistently ranks highly in evaluations of services for users, it, and other academic libraries, can do still better to live up to community ideals. Other study results indicate that users find libraries confusing to use, and that they sometimes prefer the currency and quantity of Web resources on the open Internet to the carefully selected library resources. Analysis of student papers in one class revealed that student use of scholarly materials declined as their use of Web resources increased.[2]

As the information, educational, and cultural landscape has changed, so have libraries. In the past two decades the information revolution has swept the world, resulting in a vast increase in publications in all formats. Printed works are estimated at almost one million titles annually, and Internet Websites have proliferated to a staggering nine million in 2001.[3] Libraries have promoted access to materials over ownership as acquisition of items became economically and physically unsustainable. More and more collection development has become "just in time" rather than "just in case." As libraries lacked sufficient financial means to purchase materials, they turned to consortia to negotiate economical licensing of electronic resources and to facilitate and promote resource sharing. Aware that users had difficulty navigating the Internet and identifying relevant and high quality material, bibliographers and reference librarians began to create Web pages of recommended sites and gateways to both free and proprietary resources. Often these Web sites and online subject guides have been the product of a single, highly motivated individual. Although there are many examples of collaborative initiatives, there are many more examples of locally produced sites tailored to campus needs. This approach demonstrates the fertility and originality of their progenitors, but it can produce a fragmented and redundant collection of resources. Pitschmann, in his 2001 work entitled *Building Sustainable Collections of Free Third-Party Web Resources*, estimates that subject pages and guides on library sites exhibit overlap of 75% or higher from library to library.[4] For the scholar for whom local boundaries diminish in importance as she undertakes multidisciplinary, multi-institutional research, these shortcut sites are a welcome, but inadequate, tool. From the library administrator's perspective, these Web pages are an expensive investment of time to produce and costly to maintain. There is often little tracking or assessment of their use or value, and they may lack sophisticated design or usability planning. Depending on the technical proficiency of the subject specialist and the priority he gives to facilitated access to electronic materials, some domains may not even have the support of a local Web page of resources. The result is often a spotty, uncoordinated montage of resources that lack the traditional organizational rigor of the library catalog or the exuberant diversity returned through a search engine such as Google.

Libraries today are undergoing significant transformation in their organization and in their host culture, but there are strong forces preserving a propensity to think locally. The majority of practitioners entered the workforce when the ownership model was dominant. As they have an important constituency in faculty who share many of the same predispositions, it is difficult to change past practices. Attitudes and expectations shaped in one environment affect willingness to adopt new models. Cooperative collection development, for example, is an idea which has endured much testing over the past fifty years. Many bibliographers, responding to the long-standing preference of library users to have material available for onsite browsing, have a somewhat jaundiced view of cooperative collection building, especially when conducted at the national or international level.

An early and much cited example of cooperative collection development is the Farmington Plan, initiated in 1948 in the post World War II period of international engagement. American research libraries volunteered to collect publications from designated countries or regions, with the objective of building comprehensive, nationally distributed collections that would be expeditiously cataloged and available to scholars through interlibrary loan. The Farmington Plan never achieved its full promise, as the voluntary arrangement and the acquisition of materials that were not always a local priority undercut its effectiveness. With the added burden of manual, original cataloging and the barrier of physical distribution through interlibrary loan, the Farmington Plan was abandoned in the 1960s.[5]

In the mid-1970s, the Research Libraries Group (RLG) came into existence with the goals of shared cataloging, shared collection development, shared resources, and shared preservation. A major tool for collection analysis was the conspectus, which was designed to assist libraries in balancing their collecting responsibilities on a national scale. Despite the value of the conspectus in assessing collection strengths and in creating a framework for cooperative collection development, true distribution of collecting among RLG libraries did not occur at the ideal level envisioned by its members. Again, libraries were loath to forego purchasing titles for local use in order to collect more deeply in a subject or area for the national good. By the 1990s RLG had shifted its emphasis to collection access, rather than coordinated collection development, and no longer maintained the conspectus. The overhead of coordination along with the precedence of local interests over the common good overwhelmed the original intentions.[6] More recently the Association of Research Libraries, with the encouragement of the Association of American Universities and support from The Andrew W. Mellon Foundation, has developed the Global Resources Program. This voluntary initiative has embraced a variety of different approaches aimed at expanding access to foreign publications. It includes a cooperatively developed table of contents database, coordinated collection development with commitments to collect publications from specific countries at a national level, and creative resource sharing agreements.[7] The Global Resources Program has continued to expand and to increase its utility for participants, but it has not yet had a sweeping transformation of research libraries' collecting behavior. Bibliographers still struggle to acquire as much material as possible for local ownership. The policies and practices for physical acquisition often carry over into their thinking about access to digital materials. Local considerations hold the greatest weight, and cooperation occurs on the margins of behavior.

Branin, Groen, and Thorin, writing on the changing nature of collection management in research libraries, posit that information technology will create a new model of scholarly communication, and that the effect of the digital revolution will be to foster a "shift from a decentralized system of duplicate print collections to one of fewer central repositories."[8] They describe the contribution of economic constraints and digital information systems to the reshaping of collection management, as publication inflation (in number and in cost) and competing endeavors such as the rise of big science have created enormous challenges for traditional operations. They characterize the emergence of Web resources as an untamed phenomenon. Significant new categories of material, perhaps a manifestation of gray literature, but with far more import than their print cousins because of the ease with which any researcher connected to the Internet can find them, present a wide-open field for collection management. The authors observe that over 20 years ago Charles Osburn envisioned collection development as having two fundamental stages, the first, in which the local constituency would be served, and the second, which would integrate local efforts into a cohesive national resource sharing system. In the print world, librarians achieved only an imperfect movement toward the second stage, hindered by physical barriers where geography played a significant part in defining focus.[9] Osburn in turn cites the visions of library leaders William Warner Bishop and Verner Clapp, who both predicted a new mode for libraries that would transcend local, physical limitations. Bishop, in 1940, anticipated that in 30 years, all material in the U.S. would be within reach in a reasonable amount of time, and Clapp in 1964 foresaw the need for radical restructuring of library operations to cope with the rising growth in publishing activity.[10] Electronic resources and the ready ability to transform analog materials into digital documents create powerful opportunities for librarians to achieve "the ultimate goal: a freely accessible, integrated, and comprehensive record of serious scholarship and knowledge."[11]

The primary organizing elements for access to resources of interest to academicians have, until the last decade, been the library catalog and subject indexes. With the growth of the Web and the popularity of search engines, many students and scholars have rejected the standard tools in favor of Google, Yahoo, and other Internet services. The New York Times reported on this behavioral shift in August 2000, noting that: "Even though libraries are organized and easily navigated, students prefer diving into the chaotic whirl of the Web to find information."[12] Although librarians continue to invest heavily in the maintenance of their catalogs, they have recognized that they need to find new methods of providing access to a range of materials that may never reside within their walls. Pitschmann addressed the issue of non-traditional content in his monograph *Building Sustainable Collections of Free Third-Party Web Resources*, in which he outlines criteria for "selection" of materials falling into this category and describes the vulnerabilities of both the digital documents themselves and the systems for making them available.

Applying the fundamental responsibilities of the librarian to acquire, organize, provide access to and preserve literature of scholarly value to digital resources, Pitschmann proceeds from the premise that libraries need to include free third-party sites in their discovery tools such as library catalogs or authorized Web sites in order to assist scholars in locating quality materials amidst the chaff of the Internet. By applying standard terminology or description to this information, librarians further facilitate retrieval. Specific selection criteria and a collection scope note should govern the choice of materials. Among the criteria for selection are validity, accuracy, authority, uniqueness, completeness, coverage, currency, and audience. Other factors may include the design of the site, language, and site and system integrity. Pitschmann also explores the organizational and financial aspects of building and maintaining sites. When creating large, comprehensive Web sites with many resources, librarians often establish advisory boards to assist them in identifying and vetting materials. Links require consistent monitoring. There is often a need for close collaboration among subject specialists, catalogers, technical staff, and reference librarians in order to produce a reliable resource of substance and utility. Although an individual can build a subject gateway alone, it is increasingly a demanding task, as the volume of resources increases at a rate that exceeds the capability of most people. Most libraries now have pages featuring collections of electronic resources–guides, pathfinders, portals, and gateways–generated with significant investment on the part of many staff. Pitschmann observes the duplication of effort, with perhaps 75% of the resources being redundant from site to site.[13]

A review of a selection of subject gateways reveals some of the challenges facing librarians and scholars. In the area of German Studies, for example, there is a voluntary collaborative effort on the part of members of the Association of College and Research Libraries Western European Studies Section (WESS) to identify digital resources of value. A bibliographer at Dartmouth College coordinates a Web site with the assistance of five other experts who monitor resources in particular sub-domains and contribute the URLs of resources on a regular basis. This is a rich site with many links and good organization, although it does not post its selection criteria or have a scope note. There is no historical information about the existence of the resource, which currently receives computer support from Dartmouth. Sampling the Web sites of the home institutions of the contributing members, the searcher learns that the WESS German Studies Web site is incorporated in local pages, although one may need to scroll through dozens of items to locate it. At one institution with an outstanding German program, the WESS site appears on a second page under the heading "Social Sciences & Electronic Texts." The alphabetical listing that begins "Avalon Project, Bobst Library at NYU, Bundesesinstitut" . . . etc., makes it relatively easy to find the resource. At another prominent university, a German Literature Research Guide provides access to a variety of print and non-print materials. The first item under the heading "Selected Internet Sources in General German Studies" is the German Studies Web.

At yet another premier institution with an active German bibliographer, there is no online guide to German Studies materials maintained by the library. Rather, the German Department itself has a Web site with hundreds of resources. A quick sampling of this colorful site reveals no discernable organization except for rudimentary categories and several broken links. Clicking on the heading "Electronic Resources," one finds "Our German and Cultural resources are also worth your time." The first link on the resulting page is for the Uni Karlsruhe Virtual Library, which has a list, again in no apparent order, of resources. The second one listed, German Studies at the University of Arizona, seems like a potential route to the WESS German Studies home page, but following this link does not reveal it among the sources listed on this departmental Web site. Meanwhile, returning to Google, the "library" of our computer scientist, and searching German Studies, the result is that the WESS site appears as the second listing. (The first is a site maintained by a faculty member at the University of North Carolina at Greensboro. It indicates it was last updated in May 2001, or seven months before the time of this search.) One concludes, from this brief excursion into the world of German Studies resources, that the environment is somewhat chaotic. Although there is effort to coordinate the identification of resources and to facilitate access for scholars, the results are mixed. Awareness of the German Studies Web appears limited in many other sites which purport to provide access to German studies. There is considerable overlap, but also surprising disparity in these sites. In many sites, the organization seems haphazard or opportunistic. Maintenance of the site is not always current. Libraries and academic departments are both engaging in duplicate effort, with no clear division of roles or evident collaboration.

In an attempt to impose greater order on the vast resources of the Web and to provide the professional organizational expertise of librarians, the United Kingdom's Joint Information Systems Committee (JISC) has created a service RDN (Resource Discovery Network) which aims to bring "the best of the Web" to scholars and students. According to its promotional literature, "The big difference between the RDN and search engines like Google and Altavista is that the Web sites are selected for you by one of our network of subject specialists. You can be certain that the sites you find will be useful, relevant to UK education, up-to-date and reliable."[14] The RDN operates with a number of hubs, which provide data about particular subject areas and specialized services. Humbul, for example, concentrates on the humanities, including German language and literature. (German politics and government appears in the Social Science Information Gateway.) It is possible to cross-search the hubs to locate information for interdisciplinary work. Selected contributors to the catalog of Internet resources include the University of York's Archaeology Data Service, the University of London's Institute of Historical Research, the University of London Library, the Oxford Text Archive, and the University of Oxford. The Web site exposes its collection development policy, defines its audience, and indicates its willingness to collaborate with other existing Web sites. It aims to achieve "critical mass" through accepting contributions from organizations and individuals and from metadata harvesting. Contributions are governed by selection guidelines that include relevance for the audience, the authority of the site, the originality of the content, and the currency and expected persistence of the site. Metadata is both descriptive and evaluative. The managers of the site operate a link-checking program semiannually and declare the right to remove contributions that no longer meet selection criteria.

A quick check of the site demonstrates that the WESS German Studies Web is not among the resources cited. Using the online submission form, the author proposes the URL, adds a brief description copied from the German Studies Web, and contributes the resource for consideration by an evaluation committee and, if accepted, cataloging. If accepted, it will appear within two weeks and the submission will be credited to the author. Approximately thirty records are added per week to Humbul. The site offers several exemplary features, including a well-defined selection policy, standard description, and ease of submission and use. It is sensitive to people with disabilities in its design and to the limitations of technical platforms. However, at this point it has not yet implemented its metadata harvesting capability, and its growth is slow. Humbul has fewer than 2,500 "live" records as of February 2002, and the RDN advertises 30,000. The ability to scale to the expectations of its user community has not yet been proven.

A very different subject-based resource, one aimed at surmounting the obstacle of scale, is currently under development under the auspices of the National Science Foundation. The National Science Digital Library is a prototypical national library for science, mathematics, and engineering education. It envisions providing access to information through a combination of selection by subject experts, public submissions, metadata harvesting, and the use of Web crawlers. One of its basic goals is to solve the scalability problem through the use of automated tools. It supports the

Open Archives Initiative and Dublin Core Metadata. The NSDL developers believe it is essential to move away from the labor-intensive model of providing access inherent in today's library operations and to use metadata harvesting and customized interfaces in order to provide information consumers with sufficient high quality Internet resources.

Taking a different path, but also striving to deliver quantity with quality results, are the advocates of the Scholars Portal. Although this initiative aims broadly at resources of value to higher education, it is of interest because of its proposal to apply the capability of the search engine to mine Internet resources and because it couples this automated retrieval feature with other traditional library services, such as document delivery. Several members of the Association of Research Libraries have invested in the search for a system that can be adapted to specified requirements, with the goal of piloting the Scholars Portal over the next two years. Its goal is to deliver high quality content, including a mixture of proprietary and free resources, access to library digital projects, plus bibliographic information already abundant in libraries such as catalogs and finding aids. Using cross-domain searching, aided by the deployment of common standards that foster interoperability, the ARL Scholars Portal initiative goes far beyond the creation of collaborative, subject-based Web sites, but its success will give a boost to the development of such sites, since it will expose redundancy from library to library and provide a framework for scholars to regard all connected resources as an integrated library.[15]

This small sample of library-driven activities to link students and researchers with resources cannot reflect the diversity of options available, but it does illustrate some common objectives and some hurdles which must be surmounted to create a tool for improved information service. In the information environment of the twenty-first century, academics require fast, flexible access to global resources. They are increasingly likely to seek and expect information from a variety of sources, and they may launch their initial source on the Internet, rather than beginning with the local catalog, as was historically their starting point. They are more likely to identify with their discipline than with their department or their university. Although they have delighted in the abundance of the Web, the serendipitous discovery of unique items, the granularity of full text, the plasticity of multimedia, their empowerment to search millions of pages in seconds, and the democratic aspect of the Internet, they are beginning to understand its deficiencies and their vulnerabilities as well. As they encounter retrieval sets of hundreds of thousands of items, sift through those of dubious authenticity, and sometimes fail to pull up the one resource they know does exist, they may be more open to a tool which enhances their productivity.

At the same time, librarians are painfully aware that search engines and catalogs bring different results.[16] The need to evaluate millions of sources has caused librarians to realize the futility of attempting to chase down resources individually, or even at the institutional level. In the 1970s the formation of the Ohio College Library Center, later OCLC, enabled universities and colleges to transform their cataloging operations through the use of copy and shared cataloging. The emergence of electronic resources, both proprietary and non-proprietary, has led to the adoption of a number of make-shift techniques that attempt to provide access to these items. Among the problems encountered have been the ephemeral nature of Web resources; the reluctance, because of the cost of cataloging and because of the sense that items entered into the catalog should describe permanent acquisitions, to add electronic resources to the traditional catalog; and the inability of bibliographers to scan the glut of literature on the Internet, particularly as they continued to cope with a rising number of titles appearing in print and other formats. Still primarily rooted in the model of local collections, selected for a local clientele, they hesitated to import wholesale resources identified by others. Cooperation and true collaboration, as the Farmington Plan or the RLG Conspectus and its coordinated plan for collection development have shown, can take fearsome investment and can still fail.

Nonetheless, the dominant trend today is one of merger and unification on an international scale. Increasingly, developments and advances are achieved through teamwork, rather than by a solitary genius. Effective and economical solutions call for shared intellectual capital and a common system. In order to meet the needs of scholars and researchers, librarians must work together to produce an integrated suite of services for information discovery. Among the services they must develop are regional depositories of physical items, shared collection building expertise, collaboratively created Web-based tools for locating information of value to academics, subject-based digital repositories, cooperative reference based on centers of disciplinary excellence, and flexible delivery options. Naturally, preservation responsibilities align with disciplinary agreements.

Focusing on the subject gateway or portal, we can highlight some of the elements that would be required for a successful implementation. There should be an organizational cohesiveness to the effort, with participants recognizing a common bond. They might belong to a particular association, such as WESS, be part of a consortium, such as the

Committee on Institutional Cooperation, be members of the Center for Research Libraries, the Association of Research Libraries, or the Digital Library Federation. The presence of a coordinating center would increase communication and compliance, which ought to be structured and not based on volunteer labor. There should be a knowledge management policy, with a scope statement and criteria for inclusion. An editorial board, drawn from participants and scholarly societies, should establish the policy and review general terms of inclusion. Standards for description should be set at a low enough threshold to permit submission from multiple levels of contributors. Metadata harvesting will be an essential component, because even a coordinated network of selectors and indexers will be insufficient to provide timely access to the growing body of world literature. Human intelligence will review and evaluate the gathered content, adding that critical dimension to increase the tightness of organization and relevance. In the democratic spirit of the Web, there will be an opportunity for user feedback on the resources, such as the Internet Scout Portal Toolkit proposes, a concept popularized on Amazon.com and eBay. This feedback, coupled with other evaluation tools, could be used to float superior resources to the top. Multilingual interfaces would be developed and expanded as the project grows legs. Another feature would be the ability for users to subscribe to receive updates of additions to the portal or to customize it to suit their individual requirements. An intermediate level between the general portal and the personalized portal would be the local library version, which might overlay particular local information such as the names of subject experts or onsite events. Branding the resource will be important, since that will convey authority and credibility, which will in turn increase its use. To ensure the broadest possible acceptance, those responsible for the subject-based portal would publicize it broadly. This would also reduce the redundant efforts currently rife in academic departments that have undertaken to describe Web resources without having this as their core mission. The site would incorporate traffic monitors and assessment tools to determine the extent and value of its use and impact and to refine its structure for increased worth.

A Utopian vision? Perhaps. The economic model for such a collaborative effort must be clarified. Does the subject-based portal operate through the circle of gifts, in which different institutions take the lead in certain disciplines, achieving an unforced load-leveling? Do we follow the net lender, net borrower model and establish compensation for net contributors and charges for users, perhaps for users outside a certain community? Is the resource collaboratively funded for the public good, either on a single or tiered dues level? Will governments subsidize it? Will the PayPal mode work, or the Public Broadcasting Pledge approach? Most collaborative efforts begin with seed money from external sources and a set of committed believers who contribute to establish the proof of concept. Around the world, there are a variety of initiatives developing that will explore different models. At present, the Internet is still in its infancy, and we cannot predict what a mature enterprise will look like.

Currently a group of libraries belonging to an informal group know as Ivies+ (The Ivy League institutions plus Stanford, Chicago, and MIT) are entertaining a proposal put forth by Michael Keller, University Librarian at Stanford, to produce collaboratively "Web-based synthetic guides to disciplinary literature." The goal would be to create online tools in the social sciences and humanities to reduce duplication of effort, produce improved pathfinders that would be more comprehensive, current, and detailed, and to inject a degree of standardization across domains that would facilitate interdisciplinary scholarship. Keller envisions locally mounted pages that would plug into the local environment and be constantly and cooperatively updated.

It is only a matter of time before such ideas precipitate and produce aggregated resources from distributed contributors. Initially, the creation of common discipline-based resources will require yielding of some individuality and local flavor. For those who believe they alone can be the arbiter of quality, they will believe that excellence will suffer. But, electronic resources are ubiquitous, and our scholars show an ecumenical taste for them. A powerful driver of change is economic necessity. Individuals and single institutions cannot adequately cover the universe of knowledge with existing resources. They must band together with others of shared purpose to divide up the workload, reduce costs, and create more useful services for their ever-expanding and overlapping constituencies. The technology which fosters the generation of electronic resources and the infrastructure which enables their dissemination is another critical factor in changing the culture of libraries and the pattern of access and use of information resources. Although we cannot underestimate the complexity of achieving collaboration, the limitations of precursor initiatives can be overcome by the new reality of global connection through the Web. Librarians must exercise leadership in expanding consistent, high quality information service through the development of collaboratively designed and built discipline-based portals.

NOTES

1. Kevin M. Guthrie, "What Do Faculty Think of Electronic Resources," ALA Annual Conference Participants' Meeting, 17 June 2001. Available at *http://www. jstor.org/about/faculty.survey.ppt.*

2. Philip M. Davis and Suzanne A. Cohen. "The Effect of the Web on Undergraduate Citation Behavior 1996-1999," *Journal of the American Society for Information Science and Technology*, 52, no.4 (2001): 312.

3. *http://www.oclc.org/oclc/press/20011004a.shtm.*

4. Louis A. Pitschmann, *Building Sustainable Collections of Free Third-Party Web Resources* (Washington, DC: Digital Library Federation and Council on Library and Information Resources, 2001), 35.

5. *Encyclopedia of Library and Information Science*, 1984, s.v. "Farmington Plan."

6. *http://www.rlg.org/conspechist.html.*

7. *http://www.arl.org/newsltr/206/grp.html.*

8. Joseph Branin, Frances Groen, and Suzanne Thorin, "The Changing Nature of Collection Management in Research Libraries," *Library Resources & Technical Services* 44, no. 1 (January 2000): 23.

9. Charles B. Osburn, *Academic Research and Library Resources: Changing Patterns in America* (Westport, CT: Greenwood Press, 1979).

10. Ibid., 92-93.

11. Branin, "Changing Nature," 31.

12. Lori Leibovich, "Choosing Quick Hits Over the Card Catalog," *New York Times*, 10 August 2000, G1, G6.

13. Pitschmann, *Building Sustainable Collections*, 35.

14. *http://www.rdn.ac.uk/publications/flyers/rdnpost16.PDF.*

15. Brian Schottlaender, "Scholars Portal: Of, By, or For?" ALCTS Presidents Program, American Library Association, San Francisco, June 2001. Available at *http://www.arl.org/access/scholarsportal/schott_ppt/index.htm.*

16. Sarah E. Thomas, "The Catalog as Portal to the Internet," *Proceedings of the Bicentennial Conference on Bibliographic Control for the New Millennium: Confronting the Challenges of Networked Resources and the Web* (Washington, DC: Library of Congress, Cataloging Distribution Service, 2001), 21-37. Also available at *http://lcweb.loc.gov/catdir/bibcontrol/thomas.html.*

Lessons from JSTOR:
User Behavior and Faculty Attitudes

Kevin M. Guthrie

SUMMARY. In an increasingly fast moving environment, the need to reach out actively for information to guide decision-making is extremely important. This article focuses on JSTOR, a not-for-profit organization dedicated to helping the scholarly community take advantage of advances in information technologies. JSTOR usage statistics and a JSTOR faculty survey will be reviewed.

KEYWORDS. JSTOR, information technology, not-for-profit organization

For those of you not familiar with JSTOR, perhaps it will be helpful to provide a brief introduction to the organization to provide context for the discussion that follows. JSTOR is a not-for-profit organization dedicated to helping the scholarly community take advantage of advances in information technologies. Its initial efforts have been focused on the development of a trusted electronic archive of scholarly journals, with a commitment always to digitize the back issues of journals to Volume 1, Issue 1, as well as a commitment to preserve the electronic versions of journals as they become available. Originally established in 1995, JSTOR has grown steadily in every sense, in number of pages available, number of institutions with access, and amount of usage, to name just a

Kevin M. Guthrie is President, JSTOR, New York, NY 10011.

[Haworth co-indexing entry note]: "Lessons from JSTOR: User Behavior and Faculty Attitudes." Guthrie, Kevin M. Co-published simultaneously in *Journal of Library Administration* (The Haworth Information Press, an imprint of The Haworth Press, Inc.) Vol. 36, No. 3, 2002, pp. 109-120; and: *Electronic Resources and Collection Development* (ed: Sul H. Lee) The Haworth Information Press, an imprint of The Haworth Press, Inc., 2002, pp. 109-120.

few categories. As of May 31, 2002 JSTOR cares for a 10 million page journal archive that includes 218 titles from 24 academic disciplines. 1,328 participating institutions from 66 countries have access to the resource. Scholars and students at those institutions accessed the resource 50.2 million times in 2001, printing a total of 6.3 million articles.

Such widespread awareness and usage of the JSTOR archive across a number of scholarly disciplines offers opportunities for studying the usage behaviors and evolving attitudes related to electronic resources. Electronic media are rapidly becoming the primary mode of communication in the scholarly community, yet this is happening at such a fast rate that we presently know very little about how those changes are impacting research, teaching and learning behaviors, much less the second order questions of how it is impacting the quality of research or the productivity of researchers. These are all important questions, and this article is not going to answer them. But we have attempted to provide an initial glimpse into user behaviors and attitudes related to electronic resources as they are reflected through use of and awareness of JSTOR.

JSTOR USAGE

Growth

As mentioned briefly in the introduction, JSTOR usage has grown steadily since the resource was first made available in early 1997. (See Figure 1.)

This fact is consistent with usage of virtually all other electronic resources of which we are aware, and so is not really remarkable in any way. One question we did think worth asking, however, was whether it seems that usage of *older* scholarly journal literature is growing at such a fast rate. That would be a marked change from the past, since no one would argue that there has been a steady increase in the use of 20, 30 and 40 year-old bound volumes on library shelves. Growth in the use of material in JSTOR might imply that there has been a change in usage patterns between paper and the electronic materials.

There are a variety of factors that contribute to JSTOR's overall usage growth. Since inception, JSTOR has been adding both content (in the form of new journals) and participating institutions. Perhaps the growth is simply a result of those additions, and not an increase in the use of older material per se. In order to control for these factors, we identified a group of colleges and universities that were JSTOR participants as of December 31, 1997. We also identified the journals that

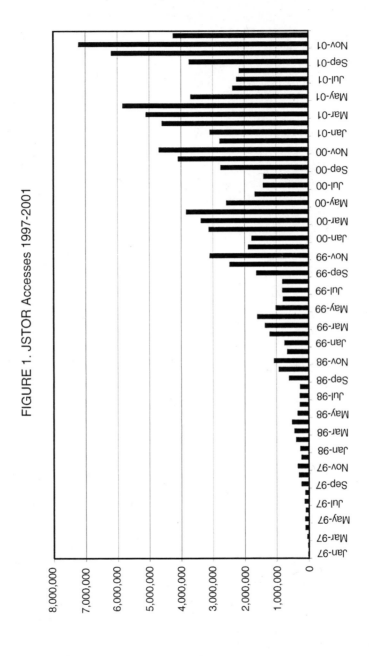

FIGURE 1. JSTOR Accesses 1997-2001

were available in the archive as of that same date. We then counted the number of total articles printed[1] at each of the participating institutions during the years between 1998 and 2001 inclusive. This offered us an opportunity to evaluate the growth rate in JSTOR use for a constant set of journals at a fixed group of institutions. Our approach does not control for growth in use that occurs as new people at a particular institution discover the resource and begin to make use of it. This is another important and interesting component of growth, but it does not confound the analysis comparing whether the journals are getting used more frequently in electronic form than they were in print.

During the period from 1998 through 2001 use of the back issues available through JSTOR grew at remarkable rates. The usage was also quite significant in absolute terms. By 2001, the average number of articles printed from a research university campus (JSTOR Very Large institutions) was 19,742 articles in a single year from the 41 journals in the study. For all sites in the assessment, cumulative growth was 425%, an estimated average annual growth rate of 62%. Clearly, use of this older literature in paper form was not of this scale and not growing at this rate prior to the materials' availability in JSTOR, or institutions would have been adding staff over the years continuously just to reshelve back volumes. There is no question that availability in electronic form is increasing use of these back issues.

Although we do not have data to explain the reasons for this growth, it is probably safe to assume that it is primarily a result of added convenience and searchability. JSTOR enables a faculty member or student to search a large database, find articles of interest, and print them out from their desktop printer. In the paper form, the method for finding and retrieving an article in a bound volume is so comparatively inconvenient as to make the material practically inaccessible.

But even if JSTOR has increased the use of back issues, one must be careful not to make claims at this early stage about the relevant value of older literature as compared to more recently published literature. For many of the JSTOR titles in the humanities, for example, electronic versions of current issues are not yet published. More generally, JSTOR was established in 1995 when there were very few networked electronic resources available. With relatively few other options, perhaps it was natural that users gravitated to it. In a sense, JSTOR represented one of the "only games in town." As new materials are increasingly made available, it will be interesting to track whether usage of older materials eventually trends to a similar relative equilibrium as existed during the print era.

Characteristics of Use

The previous data support the widely-held assumption that making materials available electronically increases use by making access more convenient. We thought it would be useful to test whether some other widely-held assumptions are supported by JSTOR usage data. The first question we asked is whether there is a close correlation between article citations and usage. In other words, are articles that are cited most often also the articles that are used most often in the JSTOR archive?

Because there are hundreds of thousands of articles in the JSTOR database, and pulling citation data on all of them is a prohibitively expensive proposition, we chose to focus on the top 10 most-used articles in three disciplines represented in the database: economics, history, and mathematics. The number of articles included in each discipline in this assessment, along with the total number of articles printed in each discipline, is shown in Table 1.

Using the Dialog service, we searched ISI's Social Sciences Citation Index for economics data, the Arts and Humanities Citation Index for history data, and the Science Citation Index for mathematics data. We pulled the total number of citations to each of these 436 articles through 2001 and reaching all the way back to the first data available. For economics the data went back to 1972; for history, 1980; and for mathematics, 1974. We then derived an average number of citations for each of the articles over the relevant time period.

We scatterplotted the average number of citations for each article against the number of JSTOR prints for that article and inspected the relationship. The relationship between citations and JSTOR prints in each discipline followed a typical growth curve with a steep initial rise in the number of prints for articles that were cited up to 200 times. These curves began to flatten out for articles that exceeded 200 citations. While these data could be analyzed using some sort of polynomial regression, there

TABLE 1

Discipline	Number of Articles	Number of Times Printed
Economics	126	235,750
History	185	97,371
Mathematics	125	15,933
Totals	436	349,054

are well known problems (e.g., multicollinearity and variance inflation) with polynomial regressions. We chose to avoid those problems by transforming the use data using base 10 logarithms. When log prints were plotted against citations, the relationship was essentially linear, so we used simple linear regression to analyze the relationships.

What emerged from this analysis is that citations do predict usage to a degree, but not nearly as much as might have been expected. There are clearly many other reasons that articles get used. The highest R-squared of the three disciplines was in the social sciences, where it was 43%, meaning that for the social sciences 43% of the variability in the number of JSTOR prints is explained by citations. The R-squared for mathematics was only 12%.

It is evident from this analysis that highly-cited articles are not necessarily the articles that are most used in a resource like JSTOR. This lack of a close correlation between these two factors contradicts typical expectations about research resources and warrants further study.

There are a variety of possible explanations for why this correlation is lower than might have been expected. Probably the most significant is that JSTOR is used for much more than research. Perhaps researchers' use of JSTOR represents a relatively small amount of JSTOR usage. Because citation data reflect the degree to which an author cites a previously published article, they represent a "research use" of an article. There are, of course, other reasons for reading and using scholarly articles than for research; for example, teaching. It is evident from the statistics data, from course web pages, and online syllabi that faculty refer their students to articles available in JSTOR. The assignment of a particular article to a 300-student class at a major university has a material impact on usage that can be seen in JSTOR statistics.

This analysis demonstrates that the most highly-used articles in JSTOR are not necessarily those articles that have been most highly cited. This result must be considered carefully. It does not confirm that a highly-cited article is not important. Nor does it necessarily indicate that an article that is rarely used has little scholarly value. What it does indicate is that the scholarly value of an article is not reflected by a single measure. This is important information for those who use citation or usage statistics to make important decisions, such as a decision to cancel a journal subscription. In the online environment we have new ways to track the value of an article compared to what was possible in the paper-based world. For some time, citations and citation impact factor data have been the primary measures used to quantify feedback on "quality." As we develop new capacities for quantifying activity in the online environment, more sophisticated rubrics will need to be developed and utilized. There will not be a "one-size fits all" approach. To use just the two factors assessed here, citation data and usage data, the degree to which an institution might be inclined to factor in one more than the other in, say, a subscription cancellation decision, will depend on the mission and objectives of that institution. A community college is likely to weigh the importance of citation data much differently than will a research university. The general point to make here is that single measures, like number of citations and/or total number of accesses to an electronic resource, do not tell the whole story about value.

Another commonly-held assumption we wanted to test was whether there seemed to be a relationship between the age of articles and their usefulness and whether that seemed to vary by academic discipline. We used the same set of most highly-used articles in economics, history and mathematics to test this assumption and this time performed a linear regression on number of JSTOR prints plotted against the age of the article.

Once again, the results challenged our expectations. In general, it can be said that there was not a close correlation between the age of the article and usage for the most highly-used articles in these fields. In other words, the most highly-used articles in JSTOR are not necessarily the most recent articles published; rather, it is widely dispersed across the chronological range of published articles. In economics and mathematics, the correlation between age and high use was virtually non-existent, with an R-squared for economics of 4% and for mathematics of 7%. In history, however, the R-squared was much higher, 47%, which represents the highest correlation among any of the regressions that we ran in this study.

It was somewhat of a surprise to us to find that the field of history was the one where more recent articles tended to show up as the most-used. At first blush, this result seemed counter-intuitive. Wouldn't historians value older literature *more* than their colleagues in other fields? On further reflection, however, this result makes sense. When one reviews the most often-used articles in economics, one sees a list of a kind of canonical group of articles on economics fundamentals like the cost of capital or monetary policy. Some of these "classic" articles might be quite old. In fact the most-used article in JSTOR's economics cluster is a 1945 article and the second most-used is a 1968 article. In the field of history, however, there are no comparable "classic" articles. The process of scholarship is fundamentally different in this field and the JSTOR usage data reflect that fact. Not only is the use of history articles distributed across a much larger number of articles, but the usage is generally more concentrated among more recently published articles.

In Summation

This superficial look at JSTOR usage reveals several interesting results, some of which run counter to expectations. Most notable is that usage and citations are not closely correlated and that the most recent articles are not necessarily the most used. In addition, substantial growth in the use of older articles has occurred seemingly as a result of the increased convenience of online availability. It will be interesting to watch, as more and more electronic resources become available, whether these results will change.

With 50.2 million accesses and 12.8 million searches conducted on JSTOR in 2001 alone, there is an almost infinite amount of analysis that can be done on the JSTOR usage statistics. We think that there is much of value to be learned that can inform the community in helpful ways. We intend to dedicate significantly more resources to this kind of work in the future and will continue to disseminate what we learn as widely as possible.

FACULTY ATTITUDES

The proliferation of electronic resources has already had a significant impact on the way the academic community uses, stores and preserves information. So far, however, there have been relatively few systematic studies conducted to evaluate how technology is affecting behaviors and attitudes among professionals engaged in the delivery and use of that information.

During the fall of 2000, with support from The Andrew W. Mellon Foundation, JSTOR retained a professional research firm to conduct an anonymous survey of faculty at institutions of higher education in the United States. The objectives of the study were to learn how U.S. academics perceive and use electronic research resources, to begin to learn about their attitudes about the current and future impact of technology on research, teaching, and their use of the library, and to gain insight into their awareness of issues related to archiving. More than 4,000 faculty completed and returned the survey.

Background

JSTOR retained Odyssey, a San Francisco-based market research firm, to conduct the study. Established in 1992, Odyssey's exclusive focus has been on studying the changing attitudes of consumers toward electronic technologies and new media. The data for the study were gathered from responses to a detailed questionnaire mailed to over 32,000 faculty members at colleges and universities in the United States. Faculty were randomly selected from a sample of over 150,000 humanities and social sciences professors obtained from a commercial service.[2] The surveys were coded so that responses could be sorted by JSTOR class, as well as by whether the faculty member was at a participating JSTOR institution. Respondents also were asked to indicate their discipline or field of study as well as the number of years they have worked as a faculty member. Most respondents did provide this information, allowing us to analyze whether responses seemed to vary by academic discipline or age of the respondent.

General Findings

First, the obvious: electronic resources are here to stay. More than 60% of faculty are comfortable using electronic resources, believe a variety of electronic resources are important to their research, and consider electronic databases to be invaluable. The resources they use most are online catalogs, full-text electronic journal databases, and abstracting and indexing databases. They expect that they will become increasingly dependent on electronic resources in the future.

One of the most important resources for faculty members is the online catalog. Over 70% of all respondents consider their library's online catalog to be "very important" to their research. However, the importance of this resource varies significantly by field. Just over 60% of the economists consider their library's online catalog to be "very important," while nearly 90% of humanists regarded it as such. In fact, for humanists, their home library catalog is the most important electronic resource to them by a large margin. In fact, based on their replies, it is as important to their research as their personal computer.

Attitudes About the Role of the Library

Faculty rely heavily on the library. When asked to rate how dependent they are on the library for their research, 48% indicated that they are "very dependent" on their library. However, this reliance is expected to decrease in the future. When asked how dependent they think they will be in five years time, 38% expect that they will be "very dependent." According to the responses, this reliance on the library is not about the library as a place; in fact, many faculty can foresee a future when they would never go in the library building. Forty-four percent thought the following statement described their view very well: "Before long, computers, the Internet, and electronic computer-based archives and databases will allow academics to conduct much of their research without setting foot in the library." These results also varied by field, as 52% of economists indicated this statement described their view very well, while only 22% of the humanists shared that view.

Along these same lines, faculty were asked to rate the importance of three broad library functions or roles. These library functions, and the percentage of faculty that rated the function as "very important" are: as a gateway or starting point for their research (65%); as a trusted repository or archive of resources (77%); and as a buyer of resources (80%). The responses varied considerably by field for the library's gateway function. Once again, humanists seem to utilize and rely on the library much more for their research. Eighty percent of the humanists rated the library's role as a starting point for research as "very important," while, by contrast, only 48% of economists considered this library role to be "very important."

Attitudes About Archiving Both Electronic and Paper Content

One interesting question related to JSTOR is whether academics will be able to trust an electronic repository in place of having paper volumes stored locally. Faculty indicate fairly strongly that they continue to want libraries to maintain paper copies. Forty-eight percent of respondents said that the following statement described their view "very well". "Regardless of what happens with electronic archives of journals, it will always be crucial for libraries to maintain hard-copy archives." Once again, the social scientists seemed to hold a different view from the humanists, as just 24% of the economists thought this statement described their view, while 63% of the humanists agreed with it. Further, most academics do not condone discarding paper back runs. More than half of the respondents (56%) indicated that the following statement did not describe their point of view: "Assuming that electronic archives of journals are proven to work well and are readily accessible, I would be happy to see hard-copy archives discarded and replaced entirely by electronic archives." Economists are somewhat more prepared to accept that possibility, with just 35% disagreeing with the statement, while 74% of the humanists had a strongly negative reaction to the statement.

Finally, faculty were asked to indicate how important it is that electronic journals be preserved for the future. Seventy-six percent indicated that the following statement described their point of view "very well": "With more and more journals becoming available electronically, it is crucial that libraries, publishers, or electronic databases archive, catalog, and protect these electronic journals." In contrast with every other case explored, where there was significant variation across disciplines, in this case, academic discipline matters does not matter at all. More than 70% of the respondents agreed strongly with the statement about the importance of electronic archiving.

In Summation

There is evidence that faculty's use, perception and attitudes about electronic resources vary considerably across disciplines, but there are several issues about which all faculty seem to agree. First, electronic resources have become an invaluable tool for research, and faculty expect to become even more dependent on them in the future. There is also near unanimous agreement that preserving electronic journals for the future is crucial. Finally, faculty do not believe that a reliable solution for electronic preservation is in place, and in general would like hard copies of journals retained to provide backup protection, although social scientists seem somewhat less concerned about this issue than academics from other disciplines.

One area where faculty attitudes seem to vary most greatly is in how they view the library and its role, particularly with respect to providing assistance with access. Humanists depend heavily on the library to assist them in seeking research materials—to act as a starting point for research, while social scientists value the library much less for this role. Moreover, it is expected that libraries will play a less important access role in the future as more and more resources can be accessed directly by faculty from their desktops. Again, this expectation is more strongly felt among social scientists than humanists.

Given how much humanists rely on and value their libraries, one cannot help but wonder if library resources are being directed toward the academic disciplines where the library's services, especially with respect to access, are most valued. In thinking about future investments in providing new access tools, libraries might give more careful consideration toward serving the constituents that value and depend on them the most.

CONCLUSIONS

Underlying these results, both the usage behavior and the faculty attitudes, is a rather simple conclusion. In an increasingly fast moving environment, the need to reach out actively for information to guide decision-making is extremely important. The tools and resources for doing so, whether they be in the form of analyzing usage logs or conducting online surveys, are available if one is prepared to invest the resources to gather and evaluate the information.

This relatively cursory review of JSTOR usage statistics yielded some surprising findings. Citations and usage data are not closely correlated. In the pre-networked environment, citation data represented the most reliable quantitative measure of journal or article "usage," and have therefore come to dominate assessments of quality in decisions related to both subscriptions cancellations and tenure. Is it time to include usage data more in these calculations? Thoughtful consideration of appropriate mechanisms for including usage data in these discussions is an important topic for further study.

JSTOR's faculty survey also yielded some surprises and offered data to confirm general assumptions. Humanists value the access assistance provided by the library much more than do their social science colleagues. It is probably safe to assume that scientists are even further out on the spectrum than social scientists. Is that true at your library? Would your library invest its human and financial resources differently if it was clear that the history faculty needed and valued your services desperately and the science faculty much less so? These are questions that should be pursued. Perhaps the most clear message that emerged from the faculty survey is the unanimous concern expressed about the importance of electronic archiving. It is time for the community to take real steps forward to address this important issue.

NOTES

1. There are many ways to use JSTOR. One can search the archive, browse the archive, view articles or print articles. For the detailed usage assessments in this article we use articles printed as a measure of use. This is an arbitrary choice but we think it reflects the fact that a user is truly interested in the article. What is important is that we have used the same measure throughout these assessments.

2. It is important to note that, because JSTOR did not at the time include a substantial number of journals from the sciences, faculty in the hard sciences were not included in the survey.

Index

Page numbers followed by an italicized "n" indicate notes.

Integrating Total Quality Management in a Library Setting, edited by Susan Jurow, MLS, and
Susan B. Barnard, MLS (Vol. 18, No. 1/2, 1993). *"Especially valuable are the librarian
experiences that directly relate to real concerns about TQM. Recommended for all professional
reading collections." (Library Journal)*

*Leadership in Academic Libraries: Proceedings of the W. Porter Kellam Conference, The
University of Georgia, May 7, 1991,* edited by William Gray Potter (Vol. 17, No. 4, 1993). *"Will
be of interest to those concerned with the history of American academic libraries." (Australian
Library Review)*

Collection Assessment and Acquisitions Budgets, edited by Sul H. Lee (Vol. 17, No. 2, 1993).
*Contains timely information about the assessment of academic library collections and the
relationship of collection assessment to acquisition budgets.*

Developing Library Staff for the 21st Century, edited by Maureen Sullivan (Vol. 17, No. 1, 1992).
*"I found myself enthralled with this highly readable publication. It is one of those rare
compilations that manages to successfully integrate current general management operational
thinking in the context of academic library management." (Bimonthly Review of Law Books)*

Vendor Evaluation and Acquisition Budgets, edited by Sul H. Lee (Vol. 16, No. 3, 1992). *"The
title doesn't do justice to the true scope of this excellent collection of papers delivered at the
sixth annual conference on library acquisitions sponsored by the University of Oklahoma
Libraries." (Kent K. Hendrickson, BS, MALS, Dean of Libraries, University of
Nebraska-Lincoln) Find insightful discussions on the impact of rising costs on library budgets
and management in this groundbreaking book.*

The Management of Library and Information Studies Education, edited by Herman L. Totten,
PhD, MLS (Vol. 16, No. 1/2, 1992). *"Offers something of interest to everyone connected with
LIS education–the undergraduate contemplating a master's degree, the doctoral student
struggling with courses and career choices, the new faculty member aghast at conflicting
responsibilities, the experienced but stressed LIS professor, and directors of LIS Schools."
(Education Libraries)*

*Library Management in the Information Technology Environment: Issues, Policies, and Practice
for Administrators,* edited by Brice G. Hobrock, PhD, MLS (Vol. 15, No. 3/4, 1992). *"A road
map to identify some of the alternative routes to the electronic library." (Stephen Rollins,
Associate Dean for Library Services, General Library, University of New Mexico)*

Managing Technical Services in the 90's, edited by Drew Racine (Vol. 15, No. 1/2, 1991).
*"Presents an eclectic overview of the challenges currently facing all library technical services
efforts. . . . Recommended to library administrators and interested practitioners." (Library
Journal)*

Budgets for Acquisitions: Strategies for Serials, Monographs, and Electronic Formats, edited by
Sul H. Lee (Vol. 14, No. 3, 1991). *"Much more than a series of handy tips for the careful
shopper. This [book] is a most useful one–well-informed, thought-provoking, and authoritative."
(Australian Library Review)*

Creative Planning for Library Administration: Leadership for the Future, edited by Kent
Hendrickson, MALS (Vol. 14, No. 2, 1991). *"Provides some essential information on the
planning process, and the mix of opinions and methodologies, as well as examples relevant to
every library manager, resulting in a very readable foray into a topic too long avoided by many
of us." (Canadian Library Journal)*

Strategic Planning in Higher Education: Implementing New Roles for the Academic Library,
edited by James F. Williams, II, MLS (Vol. 13, No. 3/4, 1991). *"A welcome addition to the
sparse literature on strategic planning in university libraries. Academic librarians considering
strategic planning for their libraries will learn a great deal from this work." (Canadian Library
Journal)*

Personnel Administration in an Automated Environment, edited by Philip E. Leinbach, MLS (Vol. 13, No. 1/2, 1990). *"An interesting and worthwhile volume, recommended to university library administrators and to others interested in thought-provoking discussion of the personnel implications of automation." (Canadian Library Journal)*

Library Development: A Future Imperative, edited by Dwight F. Burlingame, PhD (Vol. 12, No. 4, 1990). *"This volume provides an excellent overview of fundraising with special application to libraries. . . . A useful book that is highly recommended for all libraries." (Library Journal)*

Library Material Costs and Access to Information, edited by Sul H. Lee (Vol. 12, No. 3, 1991). *"A cohesive treatment of the issue. Although the book's contributors possess a research library perspective, the data and the ideas presented are of interest and benefit to the entire profession, especially academic librarians." (Library Resources and Technical Services)*

Training Issues and Strategies in Libraries, edited by Paul M. Gherman, MALS, and Frances O. Painter, MLS, MBA (Vol. 12, No. 2, 1990). *"There are . . . useful chapters, all by different authors, each with a preliminary summary of the content–a device that saves much time in deciding whether to read the whole chapter or merely skim through it. Many of the chapters are essentially practical without too much emphasis on theory. This book is a good investment." (Library Association Record)*

Library Education and Employer Expectations, edited by E. Dale Cluff, PhD, MLS (Vol. 11, No. 3/4, 1990). *"Useful to library-school students and faculty interested in employment problems and employer perspectives. Librarians concerned with recruitment practices will also be interested." (Information Technology and Libraries)*

Managing Public Libraries in the 21st Century, edited by Pat Woodrum, MLS (Vol. 11, No. 1/2, 1989). *"A broad-based collection of topics that explores the management problems and possibilities public libraries will be facing in the 21st century." (Robert Swisher, PhD, Director, School of Library and Information Studies, University of Oklahoma)*

Human Resources Management in Libraries, edited by Gisela M. Webb, MLS, MPA (Vol. 10, No. 4, 1989). *"Thought provoking and enjoyable reading. . . . Provides valuable insights for the effective information manager." (Special Libraries)*

Creativity, Innovation, and Entrepreneurship in Libraries, edited by Donald E. Riggs, EdD, MLS (Vol. 10, No. 2/3, 1989). *"The volume is well worth reading as a whole. . . . There is very little repetition, and it should stimulate thought." (Australian Library Review)*

The Impact of Rising Costs of Serials and Monographs on Library Services and Programs, edited by Sul H. Lee (Vol. 10, No. 1, 1989). *". . . Sul Lee hit a winner here." (Serials Review)*

Computing, Electronic Publishing, and Information Technology: Their Impact on Academic Libraries, edited by Robin N. Downes (Vol. 9, No. 4, 1989). *"For a relatively short and easily digestible discussion of these issues, this book can be recommended, not only to those in academic libraries, but also to those in similar types of library or information unit, and to academics and educators in the field." (Journal of Documentation)*

Library Management and Technical Services: The Changing Role of Technical Services in Library Organizations, edited by Jennifer Cargill, MSLS, MSed (Vol. 9, No. 1, 1988). *"As a practical and instructive guide to issues such as automation, personnel matters, education, management techniques and liaison with other services, senior library managers with a sincere interest in evaluating the role of their technical services should find this a timely publication." (Library Association Record)*

Management Issues in the Networking Environment, edited by Edward R. Johnson, PhD (Vol. 8, No. 3/4, 1989). *"Particularly useful for librarians/information specialists contemplating establishing a local network." (Australian Library Review)*

Acquisitions, Budgets, and Material Costs: Issues and Approaches, edited by Sul H. Lee (Supp. #2, 1988). *"The advice of these library practitioners is sensible and their insights illuminating for librarians in academic libraries." (American Reference Books Annual)*

Pricing and Costs of Monographs and Serials: National and International Issues, edited by Sul H. Lee (Supp. #1, 1987). *"Eminently readable. There is a good balance of chapters on serials and monographs and the perspective of suppliers, publishers, and library practitioners are presented. A book well worth reading." (Australasian College Libraries)*

Legal Issues for Library and Information Managers, edited by William Z. Nasri, JD, PhD (Vol. 7, No. 4, 1987). *"Useful to any librarian looking for protection or wondering where responsibilities end and liabilities begin. Recommended." (Academic Library Book Review)*

Archives and Library Administration: Divergent Traditions and Common Concerns, edited by Lawrence J. McCrank, PhD, MLS (Vol. 7, No. 2/3, 1986). *"A forward-looking view of archives and libraries. . . . Recommend[ed] to students, teachers, and practitioners alike of archival and library science. It is readable, thought-provoking, and provides a summary of the major areas of divergence and convergence." (Association of Canadian Map Libraries and Archives)*

Excellence in Library Management, edited by Charlotte Georgi, MLS, and Robert Bellanti, MLS, MBA (Vol. 6, No. 3, 1985). *"Most beneficial for library administrators . . . for anyone interested in either library/information science or management." (Special Libraries)*

Marketing and the Library, edited by Gary T. Ford (Vol. 4, No. 4, 1984). *Discover the latest methods for more effective information dissemination and learn to develop successful programs for specific target areas.*

Finance Planning for Libraries, edited by Murray S. Martin (Vol. 3, No. 3/4, 1983). *Stresses the need for libraries to weed out expenditures which do not contribute to their basic role–the collection and organization of information–when planning where and when to spend money.*

Planning for Library Services: A Guide to Utilizing Planning Methods for Library Management, edited by Charles R. McClure, PhD (Vol. 2, No. 3/4, 1982). *"Should be read by anyone who is involved in planning processes of libraries–certainly by every administrator of a library or system." (American Reference Books Annual)*